THE

QUARTERLY

EDITED BY

GORDON LISH

This magazine continues to call out
for the connivance of every writer not
in sight. Come show yourself to us—
with work to make the naysayer break
a blood vessel saying his nay.
Or hers.

THE
QUARTERLY

11 / FALL 1989

VINTAGE BOOKS

A DIVISION OF RANDOM HOUSE

NEW YORK

THE QUARTERLY (ISSN: 0893-3103) IS EDITED BY GORDON LISH
AND IS PUBLISHED MARCH, JUNE, SEPTEMBER, AND DECEMBER
FOR $32 THE YEAR ($47 IN CANADA) BY VINTAGE BOOKS,
A DIVISION OF RANDOM HOUSE, INC., 201 EAST 50TH STREET,
NEW YORK, NY 10022. APPLICATION TO MAIL AT SECOND-CLASS
POSTAGE RATES IS PENDING AT NEW YORK, NY, AND AT ADDITIONAL
MAILING OFFICES. SEND ORDERS AND ADDRESS CHANGES TO
THE QUARTERLY, VINTAGE BOOKS, SUBSCRIPTION DEPARTMENT,
TWENTY-EIGHTH FLOOR, 201 EAST 50TH STREET, NEW YORK, NY 10022.
BACK ISSUES MAY BE PURCHASED, BY CHECK OR MONEY ORDER,
AT $7.95 THE COPY; ADD $1.50 FOR POSTAGE AND HANDLING
OF EACH COPY REQUESTED.

THE QUARTERLY WELCOMES THE OPPORTUNITY TO READ WORK
OF EVERY CHARACTER, AND IS ESPECIALLY CONCERNED TO KEEP
ITSELF AN OPEN FORUM. MANUSCRIPTS MUST BE ACCOMPANIED
BY THE CUSTOMARY RETURN MATERIALS, AND SHOULD BE ADDRESSED
TO THE EDITOR, THE QUARTERLY, 201 EAST 50TH STREET,
NEW YORK, NY 10022. THE QUARTERLY MAKES THE UTMOST EFFORT
TO OFFER ITS RESPONSE TO MANUSCRIPTS NO LATER THAN ONE WEEK
SUBSEQUENT TO RECEIPT. OPINIONS EXPRESSED HEREIN ARE NOT
NECESSARILY THOSE OF THE EDITOR OR OF THE PUBLISHER.

ISBN: 0-679-72173-8

DESIGN BY ANDREW ROBERTS
MANAGEMENT BY DENISE STEWART AND ELLEN F. TORRON

WRITERS THINKING OF APPLYING TO THE QUARTERLY NEED NOT
BE DETERRED BY THE BULK, OR LACK OF IT, OF MANUSCRIPT.
TO BE SURE, THE MAGAZINE HAS ONLY SO MANY PAGES BETWEEN ITS
COVERS, AND A CERTAIN NUMBER OF THESE PAGES WILL ALWAYS BE
TAKEN UP BY THIS PAGE, THE OTHER FRONT-MATTER PAGES, THE NACE
PAGES, AND SO ON. BUT THESE FIXED CONSIDERATIONS ASIDE,
THE QUARTERLY IS ENTIRELY PREPARED TO TURN ITSELF INSIDE OUT,
IF THIS IS WHAT IT MUST DO, IN ORDER FOR IT TO ACCOMMODATE
A WORK OF EXCEPTIONALLY MANY PAGES, OR OF JUST ONE. ALL TO SAY
THAT WHAT MATTERS TO THE QUARTERLY IS HOW MOST WE MIGHT
MAKE OURSELVES MATTER TO WRITERS AND TO READERS.

THE QUARTERLY

11 / FALL 1989

THE QUARTERLY

THE QUARTERLY

I had children to
watch me die

Field Events

Kyle and Kale, brothers, hid behind rocks down by the river and watched the big man swim against the current, upriver, into the rapids. The big man was pulling a canoe behind him, and the canoe was loaded with darkened cast-iron statues; a green canoe, and the big man was young. He was the largest man the brothers had ever seen. The river was the Sacandaga, which ran past their town, Glens Falls, in north-eastern New York. It was summer, and the brothers had been down on a gravel bar, washing their car with river water and sponges, when the big man had come around the bend in the river, swimming, pulling the canoe full of heavy statues. He was swimming the butterfly stroke, leaping free of the water and then crashing down, lunging.

The brothers were strength-men themselves—discus throwers and shot-putters—and they tried to follow, running along the rocky and brushy shore, calling for the big man to stop, but he swam away from them, continued up the river, swimming hard against the force of the rapids, and he left them behind, left them alone.

That night, at home, each brother in his room, looking up at the ceiling, trying to sleep, each could feel his heart beating wildly, thrashing around in his chest, and the brothers knew that the big man was up to something, something massive, something that had never been done before: they could tell just by the way their hearts were pounding that he was out there, doing something.

The wild beating in the brothers' hearts would not stop. They got up and met, as if by plan, in the kitchen, for a beer, a sandwich. They ate almost constantly, always trying to build more muscle. Sometimes they acted like twins, thought the same thing at the same time. It was a warm night, past midnight, and when they had finished their beer and sandwiches, they went outside and stood in the middle of the street under a streetlamp and looked around like watchdogs, trying to understand why their hearts were racing.

So young! So young!

They drove an old blue Volkswagen Beetle. Sometimes, when the excitement of the night and of their strength and youth was too much, they would pick the automobile up from either end like porters, pallbearers, and they would carry it around the block for exercise, trying to go all the way around the block without having to stop and set it down and rest. If anyone had been awake to look out a window, it would have looked as if the car were a ghost car flying low. But that night, after seeing the man swimming, the brothers' hearts were running too fast just to walk the car. They lay down in the cool grass in the yard, beneath elm trees, and listened to the wind that blew from the mountains on the other side of the river, and across the river, and across the valley, and up into their neighborhood; across their bodies.

Sometimes the brothers would go wake their sisters and would bring them outside into the night, and then the four of them would sit under the largest elm and tell stories and plan things. Sometimes Sukie and Soozie, the sisters, would paint their toenails while the brothers talked. That wind; each night, it seemed it would never blow again. Nothing was ever coming back—not even things that were supposed to.

The father was Heck; the mother, Louella. Heck was the principal of the local school. Sukie was thirty-four, a teacher, and beautiful: she was tiny, black-haired, black-eyed, with a wild, high laugh, a deep chest, and she had long, sweeping eyelashes, but not much of a chin. Soozie was fifteen, but already half a foot taller than Sukie, red-haired and freckled. She had wide shoulders and played field hockey; the brothers called her Soozie the Red. The reason Sukie still lived at home was that she loved her family. She simply could not leave.

Sukie was not allowed to teach at the school where her father was principal, so she taught in a little mountain town about thirty miles north, Warrensburg. She hated the job. The children had no respect, no love, and they bred with each other, drank, and died in fiery crashes, or were abused by their parents, or got cancer; they had no luck. Sukie's last name, her family's name, was Iron, and one night the boys at her school had scratched with knives onto every desktop in the school the words "I fucked Miss Iron." Sometimes the boys touched her from behind when she was walking in the crowded halls.

The night the brothers' hearts beat so wildly, they lay in the grass for a while, and then went and got their sisters. Sukie was barely able to come out of her sleep, but followed the brothers anyway, holding Kale's hand as if sleepwalking, letting him lead her out into the yard, and she sat down with her back against the tree and dozed in and out of deep fatigue, still exhausted from the school year, though Soozie was wide awake and sat cross-legged, leaning forward, listening.

"We saw a big man today," Kyle said, leaning forward and plucking at stems of grass, then putting them in his mouth and chewing on them for their sweetness, like a cow or a bull grazing. Kale was leaning forward, too, with one leg stretched out in front of him, doing hurdler's stretches. There was no moon, only stars through the trees.

"Summer," mumbled Sukie, in her half-sleep. Often she talked in her sleep and had nightmares.

"Who was your first lover?" Kale asked, grinning, speaking in a low voice, trying to trick her.

Soozie covered her ears and whispered, "Sukie! No! Wake up! Wake up! Don't say it!"

The brothers were insanely jealous of all of Sukie's boyfriends, though there had not been any for a long time.

"Michael," Sukie mumbled uncomfortably. "No, no, Arthur—no, wait, Richard, William? No—Mack, no, Jerome, Atticus, no, that caster-boy—no, wait . . ."

Slowly, Sukie opened her eyes, smiling at Kale, teasing. "Got you," she said.

Kale shrugged, embarrassed. "I just want to protect you."

Sukie smiled with sleepy, narrowed eyes. "Right."

"We saw this big man today," Kyle said. "He was pulling a boat—he was really pulling it."

Night, like a blanket, falling all around them. Everything was new. Nothing would ever be old. There was only the future. There had never been a past.

They saw him a week later, in a pasture north of their town. The three of them—Kyle, Kale, and Soozie—were driving, going nowhere, late in the afternoon; they were over into Vermont and had taken a back road, for no known reason—they were merely exploring. Blackbirds flew up out of the marsh reeds along either side of the road. They passed old crumbling stone farmhouses, crumbling stone walls, and stopped the car when they came to the pasture he was in.

There was a large two-story stone house at the edge of the pasture, like a castle, with a stream out front shaded by elm trees, the pasture deep with rich green summer hay, and there were a few half-domestic cattle—black-and-white Guernseys—grazing in the hay.

The man wasn't wearing anything, and he had one of the cows on his back; he was running through the tall grass with it, leaping sometimes, for no reason—doing awkward *tours jetés,* awkward but heartfelt pirouettes with the sagging cow draped across his wide shoulders. He had thick legs that jiggled as he ran, and he looked happy, as happy as they had ever seen anyone look.

The rest of the herd stood in front of the old house, grazing and watching without much interest—but the big man was whirling and dancing, with that one cow on his back, and he was running first to one end of the pasture and then the next—never disappearing—sometimes running off into the woods, but even then they could still see him running through the trees, a flash of pale, back in the woods.

"Jiminy," said Soozie, thinking immediately, somehow of her sister, of Sukie, and of Sukie's laugh.

"Let's get him," said Kyle, the oldest, the strongest. "Let's wait until he goes to sleep and then tie him up and bring him home. I want to try it."

"We'll teach him to throw the discus," said Kale.

"If he doesn't want to throw the discus, we'll let him go," said Kyle. "We won't force him to."

"Right," said Kale.

But force wasn't necessary. They went out into the field after him, warily, but he stopped spinning and shook hands with them (Soozie stayed in the car, wanting to look away but unable to: she watched the man's face, watched the cow on his back), and the big man grinned, laughed, crouched, and put the cow back on the ground, and told them that he would like to learn to throw the discus, that he had never done it, had never even seen it done, but would like to try, if it was what they wanted him to do. He left them and went into the old stone house for a pair of jeans and tennis shoes and a white T-shirt. He looked larger when he came back out, dressed.

He was too big to fit into the car—he was as tall as Kyle but thirty pounds heavier, and rock-slab muscle—so he rode standing on the back bumper, grinning, with the wind blowing his long, already-thinning hair back behind him. The big man's face was young, his skin smooth and tanned.

"My name's A.C.!" he shouted to them as they puttered down the road. Soozie leaned her head out the window and looked back at him, wanting to make sure he was all right. The little car's engine shuddered and shook beneath him, trying to manage the strain, taking them up the hills and then coasting down with the back bumper scraping the road, dragging.

"I'm Soozie!" she shouted. "Kyle's driving! Kale's not!"

Her hair swirled and snarled around her, a nest of red. She

knew what Sukie would say. Sukie thought that all the muscle on her brothers was frou-frou, adornment, unnecessary. Soozie hoped Sukie would change her mind.

"Soozie! Get back in the car!" Kyle shouted, looking in the rearview mirror; but she couldn't hear him. She was leaning farther out the window, reaching for A.C.'s thick wrist, and then higher, gripping his melon-like arm.

"She's mad!" Kale howled, disbelieving, but not the least bit jealous for some reason. "She's lost her mind!"

A.C. grinned and held on to the car's roof, taking the bumps with his legs, holding on as if for dear life, but unafraid.

When they drove up to their house, Sukie had awakened from her nap and was sitting out on the picnic table in her shorts and a halter top, drinking from a bottle of red wine and painting her toenails again; she burst into laughter when she saw them come driving up with A.C. riding the back bumper as if he had hijacked them, almost choking with laughter at his great size.

"Three peas in a pod!" she cried. She danced down from the table and out to the driveway to meet him, to shake his huge hand, and to look at him.

It was as if there were three brothers.

From the kitchen window, Louella, the mother, fifty-eight years old, watched, horrified. The huge young man in the front yard was not hers. He might think he was; and everyone else might, too—but he wasn't, she could tell, and she stopped drying dishes and was alarmed, almost frantic at the size of him, standing out there among her children, right among them, shaking hands, moving around in their midst. She had had one miscarriage twenty years ago. This one could have been that child, could even have been that soul.

It wanted to come back. It wanted to come home.

But this big man was not hers. Louella felt the blood draining from her face, her hands, and thought she was dying.

She fell to the kitchen floor in a faint, breaking the coffee cup she was drying.

It was the end of June. All over the Hudson Valley, fields and pastures were green. She had been worrying about Sukie's sadness all through the fall and winter, on through the rains and melting snows of spring, and even now, into the ease of green summer.

She sat up groggily and adjusted her glasses; then rose and cleaned up the broken cup.

When she went outside to meet A.C., she could no longer say for sure whether she knew him or not; there was just that moment's hesitancy, and all the other children were so happy around him.

She looked hard into his eyes, and dried her hands on her apron once more and reached out and shook his big hand, suspecting that he did not belong but unable, at that last second, to say it. She was swayed by her children's happiness. There was a late-day breeze on all of them. A hummingbird dipped at the nectar feeder on the back porch. It was only June. She gave herself up to him, to the doubt of him, and let him come into their house. Her house.

"We're going to teach A.C. to throw the discus," said Kale.

"Thrilling," said Sukie.

Everyone followed A.C. and the brothers into the house.

He had supper with the family, and they all played Monopoly that evening. Louella asked A.C. where he was from and what he did, but he would only smile and say that he was here to throw the discus. He wasn't rude, he simply wouldn't tell her where he was from; it was almost as if he did not know, did not understand the question.

They played Monopoly until it was time for bed. The brothers took him for a walk through the neighborhood, and they went all the way into town, stopping to pick up people's cars occasionally, the three of them lifting together.

There was a statue of Nathan Hale in the town square, and drunk on the new moon, drunk with his new friends, A.C. waded out through the shrubbery and crouched down below the statue and gave the cold metal a bear hug and then began twisting, rocking back and forth, pulling the statue from the ground, groaning and squeezing and lifting with his back and legs, his face turning redder and redder, rocking until he finally worked it loose, and he stood up with it, sweating, grinning, holding it against his chest as if it were a dance partner or a dressmaker's dummy.

They walked home after that, taking turns carrying the statue on their backs, and snuck it into Sukie's room and stood it in the corner, so that it blocked her exit. It still smelled of fresh earth and crushed flowers. She was a sound sleeper, plunging into sleep at every opportunity like an escape, or like a diver looking for something dropped to the bottom of a lake, and she never heard them.

Then A.C. went downstairs, down into the basement, and rested, lying on a cot, looking up at the ceiling with his hands behind his head. Kyle and Kale stood up in the kitchen by themselves, drinking a beer.

"Do you think it will happen?" Kale asked.

Kyle was looking out the window at the garden. Some nights Kyle would stand outside one of his sisters' doors, while Kale did the same thing at the other sister's door, doing nothing—just standing there in the night, just protecting them, standing watch, in case something should happen.

"I hope so," he said. "I think it would be good for her." He finished his beer. "Maybe we shouldn't think about it, though," he said. "It might be wrong."

"Well," said Kale, sitting down as if to think about it himself. "Maybe so."

Kyle was still looking out the window. "But who cares?" he said. He looked at Kale.

"This guy's okay," said Kale. "This one's good."

"But do you think he can throw the discus?"

"I don't know," Kale said. "But I want you to go find some more statues for him. I liked watching that."

That first night at the Irons' house, A.C. thought about Kyle and Kale: about how excited he had been to see them come walking up to him. He lay there in their house in the basement and thought about them—about how they looked at each other sometimes when they were talking, and about how they always seemed to agree.

Then he thought about Kyle's hair: black and short, and about Kyle's heavy beard. A little later in the night, he thought about Kale's youth: his blond curly hair, his green eyes, and the way he leaned forward slightly and narrowed his eyes, grinning, when he talked; excited about almost anything, and excited to be with his older brother, following a year or two in his wake, down the same path.

Later in the night, A.C. got up from his bed in the basement—he was sleeping among punching bags and exercise bikes, with dumbbells and barbells scattered about like toys—and he went quietly up the stairs, like a thief; past Soozie's room, through the kitchen, and into the living room.

He sat down on the couch and looked out the big front window, comfortable, legs crossed, hands clasped over his knees, and he watched the moon and clouds through the window as if watching a play, watching for a long time, dozing off for a few minutes occasionally; and around four in the morning he awoke to find Sukie standing in front of him, blocking the moon. She was dark, with the moon's light behind her lighting only the edge of one side of her face; and he could see her eyelashes on that one side. He saw her watching him very carefully, almost the way Louella had studied him.

"Look," he said, and pointed past her.

There was a wind, and outside the clouds were blowing past the moon in fast-running streams, like tidal currents, eddying, flowing, all to the same place, all hurrying past the moon, as if late to some event.

"What is that statue doing in my room?" Sukie asked. She was whispering, and he thought her voice was beautiful and was thrilled to have it directed at him. A.C. thought he could be her friend, too, as well as the brothers'. He looked at the moon, a mottled disc, important in the sky, dominant, and he wanted to protect her forever, just for her voice. He patted the side of the couch next to him.

"Do you want to sit down?" he asked.

Slowly, she did, and then, after a few seconds, she leaned into his shoulder, and put her head against it; and then put both her hands on his arm and held on.

After a while, A.C. lifted her into his lap, holding her in both of his arms as if she were an infant, or a small child, and slowly, he rocked her. She curled in against him as tightly as she could, and he rocked her like that, watching her watch him, until dawn. She had the longest eyelashes, and she tried not to blink them.

When it got light she leaned up and kissed him, quickly, touched his big face and got out of his lap and hurried into the kitchen to fix coffee before anyone else was up. A few minutes later, Louella came through the living room, sleepy-eyed, shuffling, wearing a faded blue flannel night robe and old slippers, reading the paper. She almost stepped on A.C.'s big feet—she stopped, surprised to see him up so early, and in her living room—and he stood up and said, "Good morning," and she smiled then in spite of herself.

Around eight o'clock, Kyle and Kale got up, and they chased each other into the kitchen, playing some advanced twenty-plus-year-old's game of tag—the lighter, faster Kale staying just ahead of Kyle, leaping over coffee tables, spinning, tossing footstools into his path for Kyle to trip over. Sukie shrieked, spilled some milk from the carton she was holding, and Louella shouted at them to stop it, tried to look stern, but was made young again by all the motion, and secretly loved it—and A.C., having come meekly in from the living room, stood back and smiled, watching. Louella glanced over at him and saw him smiling, watching the brothers, and she thought again of how eerie the fit was, of how he seemed to glide into all the right spots and stand in exactly all the right places: it was as if he had been with them all along—or even stranger, it was as if he were some sort of anchor weight or stone, placed on a scale of justice which balanced them better now.

She touched the side of her head, up near her temple, and sipped her coffee, and was attracted to that thought.

After breakfast—a dozen eggs each, some cantaloupes, a pound of sausage split among them, a gallon of milk, and a couple of plates of pancakes—the brothers went out to their car and threw all their throwing equipment in it—tape measure, discs, throwing shoes—and then they leaned the driver's seat forward so that A.C. could get in the back, but still he wouldn't fit.

So he rode standing on the back bumper again, and they drove to the school, to the high windy field in which they threw and from which it seemed they could see the whole Hudson Valley and the knife cut through the trees where the river ran, the Sacandaga melting through the mountains, and then, on the other side, the green walls of the Adirondacks.

A.C. stood on the bumper and looked around at the new town as they drove. He thought about Sukie, about how soft and light she'd been in his arms, and of how he'd been frightened by her. He thought about the brothers, letting him ride on the back of their car, and he wondered what throwing the discus would be like.

Riding on the back of the tiny car reminded him of being in the river, swimming up through the rapids: all that rushing force, relentless, crashing down over and around him, speeding past. It was exactly like being in the river. Things were going by so fast. He looked around and felt dizzy at the beauty of the small town.

The little Volkswagen sputtered and strained, moving them toward the field.

There was a concrete ring out in the center of the field, a flat, smooth, unpainted circle of cement, and that was where the brothers and A.C. set their things and began to dress. The brothers sat down like bears in a zoo and began taking their street shoes off and lacing up instead their heavy leather throwing shoes, stretching, leaning forward and grasping their toes, and looking out at the field, at the wire fence running along the south end of the field, which was the point they tried to reach with their throws.

A.C. put his shoes on, too, the ones they had given him, and stood up.

He felt how solid the earth was beneath him. His legs were dense and strong, and he kicked the ground a couple of times with the heavy shoes. A.C. imagined that he could feel it shudder when he kicked. He jumped up and down a couple of times: short little hops, just to feel the earth shudder again.

"I hope you like this," said Kale, still stretching; twisting his body into further and further unrecognizable shapes and positions; he was loosening up, twisting, and right before A.C.'s eyes seemed to be turning to some kind of water and flowing: it was exactly like watching the river.

A.C. sat down next to them and tried to do some of the stretches, too, but it didn't work for him yet.

He watched the brothers for half an hour, as the blue air over the mountains and valley waned, turning to a sweet haze, a slow sort of shimmering feeling that told A.C. it was summer and that perhaps, this year, always would be. Kale was the one he most liked to watch.

Kale would crouch in the ring, twisted—wound up—with his eyes closed, his mouth open, and the disc hanging back, hanging low, and knees bent; and then, when the movement started, it was like the certainty that some magical force was being born, and that no other force on earth would be able to stop the rest of it from happening.

Kale began to spin as he moved forward, staying in the small circle, hopping from one foot to the other, staying low but giving the hint of rising—and then he was suddenly at the other end of the small ring, out of room—if he went over the little wooden curb circling the ring and into the grass, it would be a foul—and with no time or space left in which to spin, he shouted, brought his arm all the way around on the spin, his elbow locking straight out as he released the disc, and only then did the rest of his body, starting with his head, react: the head snapped back and then forward from the backlash and recoil; it was as if he'd first made the throw and then had a massive heart attack.

"Wow," said A.C., still watching Kale; watching him unwind, recover, and return, surprisingly, to a normal upright human being.

But Kyle and Kale were still watching the disc. It was moving so fast. There was a heavy, cutting sound when it landed, far short of the fence, and it skidded a few feet after that and then stopped, as if it had never been moving.

Kale threw two more times—they owned only three discs—and then the three of them, walking like gunslingers, like giants from another age, walked out to get the discs, and the brothers talked about the throws: what Kale had done right, what he had done wrong. His foot positioning had been a little off on the first throw. He hadn't kept his head back far enough, going into the spin of the second throw. The third throw had been pretty good. On the bounce, it had carried into the chain-link fence.

Kyle threw next; and then Kale again, and then it was Kyle's turn once more.

A.C. watched, and thought he knew. He thought he could watch someone do it and then do it himself. Certainly that whip-spin dance, skip, hurl, and shout was a thing that was in everyone; and indeed, it was much the way he often felt when he went out into the fields and picked up a cow, spun through the tall grass holding it on his shoulders. When it was his turn, he tried to remember that, and he stepped into the ring, huffing.

A.C.'s first throw slammed into the center of the head-high fence and shook it, the fence the brothers always tried to reach, and the brothers looked at each other, trying not to feel amazed; it was the thing they thought they had known all along; it was as if he had always been with them.

But A.C.'s form was spastic: it was wrong, it was nothing. He threw with his arms and shoulders—not with his legs, and not with the twist of his wide back.

If he could get the spin down, the dance, he would throw it 300 feet. He would be able to throw it the length of a football field. In the discus, 230 feet was immortality.

A.C. was God already. He just didn't have the spin down yet. But they were sure they could teach it to him. The amazing thing about a bad spin, as opposed to a good one, is how *ugly* it looks. Because whereas a good spin excites the spectators, touches them all the way down and through—makes them wish they could do it—or even more, makes them feel as if they *had* done it, somehow—a bad throw is like watching a devil monster changeling being born into the world; just one more bad and sad thing into a world of too many, and even spectators who do not know much about the sport will turn their heads away, even before the throw is completed, when they see an awkward spin; and A.C.'s was, Kyle and Kale had to admit, the ugliest of the ugly.

His next throw went over the fence.

The one after that—before they realized what was happening—or they realized it too late, as it was in the air, climbing, moving faster than any of their throws had ever gone—rose and then sank, gliding, and hit the base of the school, and there was a crack! and the disc exploded, shattered into useless graphite shards; one second it was there, flying and heroic—and then it was nothing, just an echo.

"A hundred and ten bucks," Kale said sorrowfully, but Kyle cared nothing for the inconvenience it would bring them, being down to two discs, and he danced and whooped, spun around and threw imaginary discs, waved his arms and continued to jump up and down. He danced with Kale, and then he grabbed A.C.

"If you can learn the steps . . ." Kyle was saying, almost singing. The three men held each other's shoulders and were dancing across the field, out toward the openness of it—like children playing Snap-the-Whip, they spun and snapped and danced, jumping. Kyle and Kale had never seen a discus thrown that far in their lives, and A.C., though he had felt nothing special, was happy, because his new friends were happy, and he hoped he could make them happy again.

Riding home, riding on the back bumper, the air cooling his summer-damp hair and clothes, he leaned against the car and hugged it, like a small child, and watched the town going past in reverse now, headed back to the Irons' house, and he hoped that maybe, he hoped very much, that he could make them happy forever.

The brothers bragged about him when they got home, and everyone listened, and like Kyle and Kale, they were half surprised, but also felt somehow that it confirmed something, and so that part of them was anything but surprised.

Kyle was dating a schoolteacher, Patty—Norwegian, shy-eyed, she was as tall as he was, with freckles and a slow, spreading smile—A.C. grinned just watching her, and sometimes, when she saw A.C., she would laugh for no real reason, just a happy laugh—and while Kyle and Kale went back into their rooms to lie down and nap, A.C. went outside with Soozie and Patty to practice field hockey.

A.C. had never played any sports and was thrilled to be racing across the lawn, dodging the trees and girls, passing the

ball along clumsily but quickly; the light coming straight down
through the tops of the tall trees.

Soozie's red hair, Patty's laughs. He would live forever.

He ran and ran, barefoot, back and forth in the large front
yard, and they laughed all afternoon.

On the nights when A.C. did not stay with the family,
he put himself up in an old abandoned stone house over in
Vermont. It was about ten miles away, and there was a way he
could get there by canoeing, taking rivers and then creeks and
streams, without any portages, and though it was upstream,
that was how he went back to the stone house.

Some nights in the farmhouse, A.C. would tie a rope
around his waist and chest, tie the other end of it to one of
the rafters, and he'd climb up into the rafters and then leap
down, swinging like a pirate, spinning, and he'd hang there,
dangling all night in the darkness. He'd hold his arms and
legs out as he spun around and around in the blackness, and
it would feel as if he were sinking, descending, and as if it
would never stop.

He would tell no one where he had come from. He would
forget the woman he had left in Colorado, the one he was
supposed to have married. Everyone comes from somewhere.
Everyone has made mistakes, has caused injuries, even havoc.
The woman he left had killed herself after A.C. left her; she
had hanged herself.

In the stone house, sometimes he would sleep all night in
the harness: spinning, relaxed, drooping like a question mark,
only to awaken each morning as the sun's first light began to
come through the dusty east windows.

There were mornings when Sukie was afraid to get up.
She knew it was just common depression, and that it would
pass with time, but sometimes it seemed too much. She slept
as much as she could, which seemed to make it worse and
worse; she kept it a secret from her parents, from Soozie,

though the brothers knew, and so, she suspected, did Louella. It was a feeling like drowning, like going down with chains wrapped around her, not caring for herself, not at all, but feeling guilty about the anguish it would cause others, her family; going down . . .

But her brothers! They anchored her; and then they soothed her, passed water through her gills, made her feel fresh again, briefly, but always again. If they came down the hall and found her just sitting there in the hallway, her head down between her knees, napping, they would pick her up, carry her out into the yard—Kyle, or Kale, or sometimes both of them—and they'd hold her over their heads, with both arms, holding her parallel to the ground, like a glider plane about to be launched. They'd run through the yard, holding her up like that, banking her, making her do steep climbs and dives, making her spread her arms out wide and pretend she was flying; they held her up over their heads with their strong, never-tiring arms, and ran quickly, barefoot, through the trees, between them, around and between them.

If Kyle was flying her, Kale would race along beside them, calling out the flight tower's imaginary instructions, clearing them for takeoff, for landings, babbling nonsense, singing love songs to her until she was crying, she was laughing so hard, and so dizzy that summer when they were all home.

They would lie in the grass afterward and gasp and pant like greyhounds, and look up at the maples, at the way the light came down through them, and Sukie would have the thought, whenever she was happy, that this was the way she really was, the way things could always be, and that that flat, vacant stretch of nothing-feeling was the aberration, not the norm: and she wanted it always to be like that, and still, even at thirty-four, believed that it could be.

It was why she got sad when it went away.

Kale would roll her over on her stomach and straddle her and begin pulling her T-shirt up, to tickle her back, to see the Water Baby birthmarks; she'd gasp, indignant, and then shriek, horrified, realizing that he was taking her shirt off in the front yard: but she couldn't get up, she could only kick and scream for her mother, while Kale and Kyle shouted, "Sukie naked! Sukie naked! Everyone come see Sukie naked! Naked Water Baby for sale!"

Her screams, their laughs, would carry all through the neighborhood, through all the trees; Kale did not ever take her shirt off all the way, but loved to embarrass or shock her, to give her the little charge of fear or excitement or of anger or love the brothers seemed always to know she needed, always. They gave it to her, and were glad to do it.

A.C. and the brothers trained every day. When A.C. was staying out at the farmhouse, he would put his canoe on the little stream that ran past his house each morning shortly before daylight, and he'd let the water catch the canoe, and with the water passing beneath him, he could float all the way to Glens Falls, not ever having to paddle—just ruddering.

As if following veins or arteries, he took all the right turns with only a flex of his wrist, a slight change of the paddle's orientation in the water, and passed beneath dappled maples, flaking cottonwoods, listening to the cries of river birds, sounds of summer, and floated all the way down into the town.

The brothers threw at the school, and lifted weights in the school's basement, and went for long runs. Each had his own goal—and each wanted A.C. to throw the unspeakable 300 feet. It would be a throw so far that the discus would disappear from sight.

No one believed it could be done. Only the brothers believed it. A.C. was not even sure he believed it. Sometimes he fell down, entering his spin, trying to emulate their grace, the precision-polished whip-and-spin and then the clean release of the disc, like a birth, the discus flying wild and free into the world . . .

In the evenings, the whole family would sit around in the

den, watching *M*A*S*H,* watching the Movie of the Week—
Conan the Barbarian once—Heck sipping his gin-and-tonic,
fresh-squeezed lime in with the ice, sitting in the big easy chair
watching his huge sons sprawled on the rug, with their huge
friend lying next to them; Soozie, sitting over in the corner,
watching only parts of the movie, spending more time watching Sukie—and Sukie, sitting next to her mother, rocking
and smiling, looking at the TV screen but occasionally at the
brothers, at A.C., at all three of them with their rumps turned
to her, entranced by whatever was showing. Louella and Patty
would be knitting, sitting in chairs on either side of the only
lit lamp, catching and bobbing and tucking and weaving, the
work of needles, knitting, watching like wardens, but also like
prisoners.

The nights that A.C. stayed over, Sukie would lead him
down to the basement, would make sure that he had a pillow,
fresh sheets. Making love to him was unimaginable, and also
the greatest thought of all; he was her brothers' find, not hers,
and he had this silly throw to make first, this long throw.

Love was unthinkable—not the waist-to-waist kind. If she
gambled on it and lost, she would chase him away from the
brothers as well as herself. The idea was unthinkable.

But each night, she and A.C. met upstairs, to sit on the
couch in the living room and to nap that way, with Sukie lying
in his arms, in his lap, curled up, her head resting against his
wide chest; that was not unthinkable.

A.C. trained all through the summer. Early in the evenings, sometimes, the brothers would go out looking for statues with him; their back yard was becoming filled with them,
all of them standing outside Sukie's and Soozie's windows.
A.C. laid them down in the grass at daylight each morning and
covered them with tarps, but raised them again each evening:
long-ago generals, riverboat captains, composers, poets.

Louella kept her eye on him, suspecting, and believing in
her heart, that he was the soul of her lost son, come back in

this huge body, come home, finally; and she did not want him to love Sukie, but she did not want him to go away, either.

A.C. had never been happier. He was still throwing clumsily, but his throws were going farther and farther: 250, 255 feet; and then 260 feet.

They were world-record throws, each time he threw, but the brothers did not tell him this, and told no one else, either; it was the brothers' plot to not show him to anyone until he was throwing—consistently—the astonishing 300 feet, so that perhaps A.C.'s first public throw would not only be a world's record but so great a distance that no one would believe he was from this earth. The brothers imagined that sportswriters and fans would be clamoring after him, chasing him, wanting to take him away and lock him up and do tests on him, examine him, so that the brothers would have to have an escape route planned, a way to get him back into the woods, never to throw again, never to be seen or heard from again . . .

The plan got fuzzy at that point. The brothers were not sure how it would go after that, and they had not yet consulted with A.C., but they were thinking maybe that somehow Sukie could figure in it.

Certainly, they had told no one, not even their mother—especially not Louella.

A.C. was euphoric as the summer moved on. When he was back at his farmhouse, he would often go out into the pasture and lift a cow and dance around with it as if it were stuffed or inflated; or in Glens Falls, he'd roll the brothers' little Volkswagen over gently on its back, in the front yard, and then he would grab the bumper and begin running circles around it, spinning it like a top in the deep summer grass: no scratches. Veins would be springing out in his forehead, in his temples. Even the muscles in his cheeks would tense and flex, showing the most intricate of striations. A.C. would grin, and Kyle and Kale thought it was great fun, too, and they'd get on either end and rock the little upside-down car like a playground toy, riding on it as A.C. continued to spin it.

The summer had not softened him; he was still all hard, still all marvelous. Children from the neighborhood would run up and touch him from behind, and after they had touched him, they felt stronger.

In the evenings, the nights he stayed over at the Irons', A.C. would carry Sukie all through the house, after everyone else was asleep in their rooms and Sukie had fallen asleep in his lap. He imagined that he was protecting her, and that he was checking to make sure the whole house was safe. He carried her down all the hallways, past her parents' room, her brothers', past Soozie's; into the kitchen, and out into the garage: it was all safe and quiet.

A.C. would go out into the back yard with her, out among the statues, and then into the street, and he would walk all through the neighborhood with her as she slept.

There was a street called Sweet Road that had no houses on it, only vacant lots, trees, and night smells; he would lay her down in the dew-wet grass along Sweet Road and touch her robe, an old fuzzy white thing, and the side of her face.

The wind would stir her hair, wind coming up out of the valley, wind coming from across the river. He owed the brothers his happiness. He could never let them down.

Some nights, far-off lightning would flicker over the mountains, behind the far ridges. She slept through it all in the cool grass, exhausted. He wondered what she was dreaming. He would sit next to her, protecting her, far into the night.

Late in the afternoons, after practice, the brothers would walk to the grocery store in town, and they'd show A.C. the proper discus steps. Sukie and Soozie would follow sometimes, to watch.

It was a mile and a half to town, and they'd walk through the quiet neighborhoods, the brothers demonstrating to A.C.

in half crouches and hops the proper setup for a throw, the proper release, and he tried to learn: the snap forward, with the throw, and then the little trail-away spin at the end, unwinding, everything finished.

Kale brought chalk and drew dance steps on the sidewalk for the placement of A.C.'s feet, so that he could move down the sidewalk properly—practicing his throws; and like children playing hopscotch, ducking and twisting, shuffling forward and then pretending to finish the spin with great shouts at the imaginary release of each throw, they moved through the quiet neighborhood, ducking and sliding, hopping, jumping up and shouting, throwing their arms at the sky. Dogs barked at them as they went past, and children ran away at first, though soon they learned to follow, after the brothers and the big man had passed, and they would imitate in the awkward fashion of children the brothers' and A.C.'s throws.

Sukie could sometimes see the depression, the old part of herself, back behind her—back in June, and back in the spring, in winter; back in cold fall and old previous dry-leaved summer—but she was spinning and moving so fast, sliding across the months and moving too quickly, so quickly, away from the old stranger of sadness.

She was still sad when no one was around, but since A.C. had started hanging out with her brothers, there finally seemed to be hope; snatches of air, feelings of good air.

A.C. showed her how to hang from her ceiling: he rigged a harness in her room so that she could hang suspended the way he did in the farmhouse and spin.

"It feels better naked," he said, the first time he showed it to her, and so she took her clothes off. Sukie closed her eyes and put her arms and legs out and spun in slow circles around and around, and A.C. turned the light out and sat down against the wall and watched her silhouette against the window, watched her until she fell asleep, and then he took her out of the harness and got in bed with her, where she awoke.

"We won't tell anyone," he said. She was in his arms,

warm, alive. It made him dizzy, as if he were spinning, to consider what being alive meant.

"No," she said. "No one will ever find out."

She fell asleep with her lips on his chest. A.C. lay there looking at the harness hanging above them, and wondered why he wanted to keep it a secret, why it had to be a secret.

He knew this was the best way to protect her; and that he loved her.

A.C. stayed awake all through the night, conscious of how he dwarfed her, afraid that if he fell asleep he might turn in his sleep and crush her. He arose before daylight and crept back down into the basement, that first night, and every night thereafter, hiding the harness in her drawer.

Many evenings the family would have corn for dinner, grilled corn, dripping with butter. They sat outside at the picnic table and ate it with their hands. Night scents would drift toward them. As darkness fell, the rest of the family would move back into the house and watch the lazy movies, the baseball games of summer, and then they would go to sleep, but Sukie and A.C. stayed up later and later, as the summer went on, and made love after everyone had gone to bed, and then they would go out on their walk: A.C. still carrying Sukie, though now she was awake.

When Sukie was not too tired—when she did not need to go to bed—she and A.C. would paddle the canoe up the river to his farmhouse, with Sukie sitting behind A.C. and tracing her fingers on his wide back as he paddled. The waves would splash against the bow, wetting them both. They moved up the river slowly, past hilly night-green pastures with the moon high above them or sometimes just beyond them, and summer haying smells coming across the fields to them; past the wild tiger lilies growing along the shores, and they'd pass over into Vermont, green Vermont in the night, and A.C. and Sukie would feel weightless and free, until it was time to go back.

Rolling on the old mattress in A.C.'s farmhouse, with

holes in the roof above them and stars through the roof, stars through the cracks. No brothers, thought Sukie fiercely, clutching him and rolling beneath him, over him, beneath him again; she knew it was like swimming through rapids, or maybe drowning in them.

They would sit on the stone wall out in front of the farmhouse, afterward, some nights, before it was time to leave—and they'd watch the cattle graze in the moonlight, listening to the slow, strong, grinding sound of the cattle's teeth being worn away as their bodies took their nourishment—and Sukie and A.C. would hold hands, and sit cold shoulder to shoulder in the night, still naked, and when it was time to go, they'd carry their clothes in a bundle down to the stream, the dew wetting their ankles, their knees, so that they were like the cattle, too, as they moved through the tall grass—and they'd paddle home naked, Sukie sitting right behind A.C. for warmth against the night.

Days were not enough. A.C. felt as if it was his second life: as if the first had been denied him, and now he had to make up for the one he had missed, plus the one he was now living.

The brothers trained in the days, still, with the summer ending, and a haze over the valley below them: the brothers were throwing far over the fence, better than they'd ever thrown in their lives, and they were tanned from the long hours of practicing shirtless. The women came and watched them some afternoons—Patty, Sukie, Soozie—and the women would have a picnic while the men threw.

A.C. had stopped sleeping altogether. There was simply too much to do.

He and Sukie would go for boat rides out on Lake George, only they would not take paddles with them. Instead, A.C. slipped a harness over himself and towed her out into the lake by swimming, as if out to sea: wading out into the shallows, first, wearing the harness, bare to the waist, wearing only bodybuilding briefs; splashing, pulling the canoe along behind him, with Sukie riding in it, sitting upright like a shy stranger, a girl met in school on the first day in September—and then thigh deep, and then deeper, over his waist—up to his chest, his neck—and he would be swimming, pulling her out into the night.

Once they were out on the lake, away from shore, he would unbuckle the harness and tease her by pretending to abandon her, leaving her out on the lake without a paddle, and A.C. would swim circles around her and then submerge, holding air in his great lungs for two minutes, three minutes, three minutes and a half. There was no way for her to bring him up; she could only wait for him.

Each time, A.C. tried to stay under longer than he ever had before. It was cold and dark, but safe, quiet, at the bottom of the lake; but then, always, he would have to kick for the surface, up to the wavering glimmer of where she was, the glimmer becoming an explosion as he surfaced, gasping, and found her trying to pretend that she was not worried, not even looking at him when he surfaced.

A.C. would get back into the harness, and like a fish or a whale, a servant, he would begin her on her journey again, taking her around and around the lake: leaving a small V behind the canoe as Sukie trailed her hand in the water and looked back at the dark, blotted treeline against the night that was the restaurant-speckled shore; or she would look out ahead of her at the other shore, equally distant, where there were no lights at all.

With A.C. so close and tied to the end of a rope, and his back so wide and deep, pulling her and the boat through the water as if she were a toy, she wanted to stand up in the boat and call out, cupping her hands, "I love you." But she stayed seated and rode, and let her hand trail in the coolness of the night water. She was not a good swimmer, but she wanted to get in with him; she wanted to strip and dive in, and swim out to him. He seemed so at ease that Sukie would find herself— watching his wet, water-sliding back in the moonlight, the dark water—believing that he had become some sort of sleek sea animal and was no longer a true human, mortal, capable of mortal things.

Occasionally Sukie and A.C. would go out to the lake in the late afternoon, before it grew dark, and she would take a book; and between pages, as he continued to swim, training, growing stronger, she would look at the treelines, the shores, all so far away—sometimes a boat out on the lake would draw nearer to see if she needed help, but always she waved them away, gave the pilot of the other boat a cheery, thumbs-up A-O.K. signal—and thinking of A.C. in the water as a sea animal, a great otter-man, something not mortal, would excite the part of her that could always get excited—and when dusk came, if A.C. had been swimming all afternoon, he would finally head back into the harbor, sidestroking, looking at her, smiling a slow, lazy smile—but she did not want laziness or slow smiles, she wanted to reach out and touch him.

In the harbor, in the dark, he would climb into the boat, slippery, and would come out of his trunks, and she would undress, and they would lie in the bottom of the cool green canoe, and hold each kiss, and feel the greatness of the lake pressing from beneath as they pressed back against it, down and down, just over all that water but not quite in it. Then they would get up and sit on the wicker-cane bench seat in the stern, side by side, and lean against each other, holding hands; and Sukie found herself wishing A.C. were not so strong, and realized she wanted him to be someone else.

They would sit in the harbor, those cool nights, wet, steaming slightly from their own heat. Other boats would come slowly into the harbor, idling through the darkness back into shore, their lengths and shapes identifiable by the green-and-yellow running lights that lined their sides for safety, as they passed through the night, going home.

Sukie and A.C. would sit very quietly on the dark water in their dark boat without lights, and sometimes it seemed as if one of the pleasure boats was coming right at them; and sometimes one of the slow-moving party boats with the green lights would pass right by them—so close that they could see the faces of the people inside—but no one on the party boat saw them, and after the party boat had passed, it was somehow darker and more silent than it had ever been; and sometimes A.C. and Sukie would make love again, excited by the near-passage, the near-discovery.

They would have coffee at a restaurant on the short drive back—five or six miles from home—sitting out on a deck beneath an umbrella like tourists, looking out at Highway 9A. Sukie liked sitting with him, drinking coffee slowly, stirring milk and sugar into the coffee, cup after cup, watching the previously coal-black coffee turn into swirling, muddying shades of brown. A.C.'s weight was up to 300 pounds, more muscle than ever, but she had begun calling him "Fat Boy," and she would reach over, smiling, watching his eyes, and grip the iron breadth of his thigh and squeeze it, then pat it and say, "How are you doing, Fat Boy?"

The lake still inside her, part of it, from where they had gone in for a quick cleaning-off swim—A.C. staying right next to her, holding her up in the water with one hand as she paddled around like a baby in a public pool being taught to swim—and part of A.C. still in her, despite the swim, and she felt deliciously wild, and they'd drink coffee for an hour, until their hair was dry. Then they'd drive on home, to Louella's fright, to the brothers' looks of happiness, but looks which were somehow a little hurt, a little lost: home to Heck's mild wonderment and interest, looking up from his gin-and-tonic, his mild but strong, waiting trust, and Soozie's longing jealousy, for they would have been gone for a long time and Soozie missed Sukie.

"We're just friends, Mom," Sukie would say, whenever Louella tried to corner her in the kitchen for a cup of coffee, for questions; Louella's worried eyes, Louella's feeling that things could go wrong.

"I'm happy, too, Mom," Sukie said. "See? Look!" She set

her coffee down and danced, leaped, and kicked her heels together three times, spun around when she landed, then went up on her toes: an odd interpretation of the discus spin that A.C. was trying to learn.

"Well," said Louella, not knowing what to say or do. "Good. I hope so."

Without even speaking about it, without agreeing or discussing it, the brothers and A.C. as well as Louella began to stand outside Sukie's door in the night. They would take turns; Louella, unable to sleep, might come down the hall to find Kale already standing there, as if guarding her, with his arms crossed, and Louella would touch him on the arm, and Kale would go back to his room, he'd be able to sleep, whereas on nights when A.C. was staying in their house Kale dreamed of thunder and imagined that the house was shifting, moving.

On the nights that A.C. stood guard, he would sometimes slip into the room, where sometimes Sukie was sleeping in the harness. A.C. thought about saving her. She was so much older than he was: fourteen years older. He wanted to burn down those fourteen years he had missed, he wanted to get another try at the time that had been missed. A.C. would wind her up in the harness, winding the rope up like a rubber band, and then he would let go and wonder what it felt like to her in her sleep, all that spinning. He would lie on his back on the bed below and watch. The moon came in through the window on her face, her hair, her back, her legs; she spun wildly, spinning fast at first, her arms and legs hanging limp, in the deepest of sleeps, so that, with the moon flashing off of her, it looked as if she were in a wild dance. Her hair had been short at the start of the summer, but it was getting longer.

Sukie's spinning was silent; neither she nor the rope made any sound. A.C. lay on the bed looking up, watching her spin just above him, and he would listen carefully, and he would hear Kale clear his throat, or Kyle shift his weight, just outside the door. Sometimes, when Louella was at the door, she would sit with her back against it and hum softly.

No one knew that they were guarding both A.C. and Sukie; no one ever knew he was in the same room with her.

A.C. could barely fit on her small bed. He would doze, until just before dawn. Whoever guarded Sukie always left right at dawn, to keep Heck or Soozie from finding out what was going on—and when A.C. heard that last person leave, he would slip out through the door and hurry back down to his cot in the basement.

On nights when A.C. and Sukie went for their walks, or when he carried her through the neighborhood, they would have to go out and come back in through Sukie's window, while Louella or Kyle or Kale guarded the empty room.

Louella assumed that A.C. was purchasing all the statues at antique stores, and though the statues unnerved her a little—particularly when she caught them in the sweep of her headlights as she turned into the driveway—she grew used to their being there as long as she did not have to look at them.

She thought about the strange giant living beneath her family in the basement; the young giant who was making her daughter happy again. She felt as if a thing was both coming back and being taken from her at the same time.

When A.C. stayed in Glens Falls, he would lift himself from sleep and move around the basement, examining the rusting old weights, the rowing machines, the rust-locked exercise bikes, and the motionless death-hang of the patched and battered punching bags. He would run his hand over the old weights, smelling the forever-still air that had always been in the basement, air in which Kyle and Kale had grown up, spindly young kids wrestling and boxing, always fighting things, but being a family: taking meals prepared by their mother, going to church, teasing their sisters, growing larger, finding directions and interests, taking aim at things—that

same air was still down there, as if in a bottle, and it confused
A.C. and made him further sure that he was somehow a part
of it, a part he did not know about.

He pictured pushing through the confusion, throwing the
disc farther and farther, until one day, as if he'd never done
it before, he'd execute the skip-and-glide perfectly, and he
would be able to spin around once more after that, twice more,
and still look up after the throw in time to see the disc flying.
It would make the brothers happy, and then perhaps they
would not be brothers anymore, or at any rate not his.

It was what he wanted. It was not what he had wanted at
first, but it was what he had come to want.

He trained harder than ever with them; he listened to them
more closely, as if it were the greatest of secrets they were
telling him; and they put their arms around him, walking back
from training.

Sometimes they teased him, trying to put his great throws
into perspective.

"The circumference of the earth at the equator is 24,000
miles," Kale would say, nonchalantly, as if looking at his watch
to see what time it was, as if he had forgotten an appointment;
and Sukie would have put him up to it, would already have
given him the numbers to crib on his wrist. "Why, that's 137,-
280,000 feet," he'd exclaim.

Kyle would look over at A.C. then and say, "How far'd you
throw today, A.?"

A.C. would throw his head back and laugh; a great, happy
laugh, the laugh of someone being saved, being thrown a rope
and pulled into shore. He would rather be their brother than
anything. He wouldn't do them any harm.

Sukie and A.C. took Soozie canoeing on the Batten-
kill River, over in Vermont. It was almost fall. School was
starting soon; Sukie stayed close to A.C., held on to his arm,
sometimes with both hands. She worried that the fatigue and
subsequent depression would be coming on like a returning

army, but she smiled thinly, moved through the cool days, and laughed, and grinned wider whenever their eyes met. Sometimes A.C. would blush and look away, which made Sukie grin harder; she would tickle him, tease him; she knew he was frightened of leaving her, she knew he never would.

They drove through the countryside, past the fields lined with crumbling stone fences; past the orange tiger lilies, and into Vermont, with the old canoe on top of the VW, and they let Soozie drive, like a chauffeur, though she did not yet have her license, and A.C. and Sukie somehow squeezed into the back seat and kissed, made out, mostly to tease Soozie. Sometimes Soozie would look back at them, a crimson blush, but mostly it was just shy glances at the mirror; trying to see ahead, as if through a telescope, into the pleasure that Sukie had fallen into: Sukie ahead of her, only a matter of years.

The road turned to white gravel and dust with a clatter and clinking of pebbles, but Sukie and A.C. did not notice. They looked like one huge person wadded into the back seat; no longer even kissing but just hugging, holding on.

Sun came through the dappled windshield, flashing. It felt good to Soozie to be driving with the window down, going faster than she ever had. Meadows passed; more tiger lilies, maples, farms. Cattle. A.C. reached forward and squeezed the back of Soozie's neck with one large hand, startling her, and then he began rubbing it; she relaxed, smiled, leaned her head back.

Her red hair, on his wrist.

Down the narrow road Soozie flew, raising dust, and brilliant goldfinches flew back and forth across the road, flying out of the cattails, alarmed at the car's speed, and once, Soozie hit one: it struck the hood and flew straight up above them, sailing back off toward the cattails, dead, wings folded, but still a bright yellow color, and Soozie cried "Oh!" and covered her mouth, because neither A.C. nor Sukie had seen it; she was ashamed somehow and wanted to keep it a secret.

They stopped for cheeseburgers and shakes at a shady

drive-in in a small town whose name they'd never even heard
of. The drive-in was right by the banks of the river, where they
would put the canoe in. The river was wide and shallow, cool
and clear, and they sat beneath a great elm and ate. Soozie was
delighted to be with them, but also she could not shake the
oddest feeling: again, that feeling that there was nothing special, that it had been happening all her life, these canoe trips
with A.C. and Sukie—and that it could just as easily have been
Kale or Kyle sitting with them under the tree as A.C.

If anything, Soozie felt a little hollow, somehow, and
cheated—as if something was missing—because A.C. had only
just now shown up, this summer.

Neither of the girls had paddled before. They sat backward and gripped the paddles wrong, like baseball bats. Sukie
did an amazing thing that A.C. would never understand: she
fell out, twice. It was like falling out of a chair. She hadn't even
been drinking. Soozie shrieked. They had water fights.

Soozie had baked a cake, and they ate it on a small island.
Soozie and Sukie waded out into the cold river to pee. A.C.
laughed and turned his back and made noise against the rocks
on the shore.

"Soozie's jealous," Sukie said when they came trudging up
out of the river. Soozie swung at Sukie and missed, and fell
back into the river.

The sun dried them quickly. They stopped often. A.C.
swam ahead of them sometimes, pulling the canoe by a rope
held in his teeth.

They had a big jug of wine, and got out and walked up into
a meadow and drank from it whenever they became tired of
paddling, which was often. A.C. swam in front of or alongside
them almost the whole way. At one stop, on the riverbank,
Sukie ran her fingers through A.C.'s hair. In a little over six
years, she would be forty. Soozie watched them. A crow flew
past, low over the river, just one.

Farther upstream, they could see trout passing beneath

RICK BASS

the canoe, could see the bottom of the river, even though it was deep, because the water was so clear. Stones lined the bottom, as if some sort of old road lay beneath them.

They stopped for more cheeseburgers on the way home, A.C. at the wheel, and had Cokes in the bottle with straws. They drove with the windows down again. Their faces were not sunburned, but darker.

The brothers' looks again, when A.C. and Sukie and Soozie got home and went into the house; the brothers were immediately happy to see the big man again, as always, but then, like small clouds, something unknown crossed their faces and then vanished again, something unknown, perhaps confused.

The day before school started, Sukie and A.C. paddled up into Vermont, to the farmhouse. They were both sad, as if one of them was leaving and not ever coming back. Sukie thought about another year of school: tired before it even began, she sat on the stone fence with him, her head on his shoulder, and was sad; and he let her be sad, did not try to cheer her up with stunts or tricks or feats of strength. The cattle out in the field in front of them grazed steadily, sometimes moving right up to where Sukie and A.C. were sitting.

A.C. rubbed the back of Sukie's neck, held her close against him, but could give nothing, could not go after her. He could be kind and tender, and he could be considerate and thoughtful, and he could even love her; but she wanted something else, a rare thing, and he knew that he was common as coal in that respect, that he was afraid. He also knew that he was afraid, too, of leaving her, and of being alone.

He held her hand, ran the other hand through her hair, down the back of it, and tried not to hate himself, his fear, his imperfection. He could see it out there, like a far wall, 300 feet, vaporous in the distance. He could see it, and on good days could feel it in him, could feel he had it; but he was frightened,

35

and sometimes when he thought about it too hard, too much, it vanished, as if it was not real.

He was running out of money, so he took a paper route; and as he had no car, he pulled the papers on a huge scraping rickshaw, fitting himself with a harness to pull it. It had no wheels and was really only a crude travois, two long poles with a sheet of plywood nailed down, and little guardrails around it so that he could stack the papers high up on it.

The noise was thunderous; he had the early-afternoon paper route. All through the neighborhoods he trotted, grimacing, pulling a half ton of paper, up the small hills slowly, and then, like a creature flown down from the heavens, like some cruel-eyed bird, he would swoop down the hills, street gravel and rock rattling under the sled. He would be shouting and throwing papers like mad, glancing back over his shoulder with every throw to be sure that he was staying ahead of the weight of the sled, which was accelerating, trying to run him down. It was funny, and the people who lived at the bottoms of hills learned to listen for him, loved to watch him, to see if perhaps one day he might get caught by the sled.

But it was lonely, for A.C., with Kale back in school, his final year, playing football, and Kyle coaching. Soozie was back in school too, and Heck was still the principal; at home there was only Louella.

Usually A.C. would finish his route in the late afternoon, and then he would go back and put the sled in the garage and hose off in the back yard, his chest red from where the harness had rubbed, his running shorts drenched with sweat; he'd hold the hose up over his head and stand there in the back yard, watering himself, cooling down. Louella would watch from the kitchen window, lonely, her heart going out to him, to his strength, his strangeness; but also cautious, frightened, also a mother first. Dripping, A.C. would turn the water off, coil the hose back up, and then sit at the picnic table, silently—his back turned to the kitchen—and like some kind of dog, finished with his duties, he would wait until he could see Sukie again, could see all of them again. Louella would watch him for a long time. She just couldn't be sure. Her eyes would water sometimes, but she had no way of knowing.

Whenever Sukie got home from school—riding on a fresh burst of energy, singing, honking the horn as she pulled in the driveway, gathering her books, armloads of books and folders—A.C. jumping up, shaking a spray of water from his wet hair like a dog, and running over to open the door for her—meeting, kissing delicately—she would ask, teasing, "How was your day, dear?" It was all working out differently from how she had expected, she was fresher and happier than she had ever been.

The children at Sukie's school were foul, craven, sunk without hope. She would resurrect one, get a glimmer of interest in one every now and then, and then it would all slide back, it had all been false: that faint progress, the improvement in attitude. Sometimes she hit her fist against the lockers after school. The "I fucked Miss Iron" desks were still there, and the eyes of the male teachers were no better, saying the same thing. And the women teachers hated her, for her beauty and her youth, because she was still young compared to most of them; but she was losing both of these things, and each year she wondered if this was the year that it would all go away. It was a gauntlet, but she needed to stay close to Glens Falls and could not teach at her father's school. She had to keep going.

It was like going down the river with Soozie and A.C.; like going out into the night, dark and cool, cradled against his chest, as he carried her: like them going into each other, that spinning—except there was no sound, no promise, no future, and she knew—she could feel it as strongly as anything—that it took her too far away from him, teaching at Warrensburg each day, a place of darkness.

Perhaps he would come rescue her, she thought.

Perhaps he would view it as a great weight, a tremendous thing to be lifted and moved.

She was up until midnight every night, grading papers, preparing lesson plans, reading the barely legible scrawled essays of rage—"I wont to kil my sester. I wont to kil my bruthers"—and then she was up again at four, or sometimes at four-thirty, when she could not make it up at four, could not rouse herself from the sleepy dream of her life—she was still sleeping in the harness, hanging—but A.C. was up at four also, or four-thirty, sitting in the front room, waiting for her. He'd have coffee fixed for her, and mostly what he thought about all the time, when he was alone, was throwing 300 feet.

It meant nothing to anyone, he knew, except a scattered handful—Kyle, Kale, and maybe Sukie, and maybe even himself, Heck, Soozie—perhaps even Louella—but beyond that, it meant nothing to anyone, and he liked that. It meant it wasn't something they were likely to take away.

He continued to bring statues into the back yard. Some nights he would go out looking for them in Louella's station wagon, and would come home with two or three of them.

He had never been stronger. They would kiss: she was warm and fuzzy in her tattered old dingy-colored robe, and she'd be wearing her owl reading glasses, not her contacts; his hands would slide up under her robe, and she'd be breathing, warm, hard, and firm, when she was young, and he wanted nothing else for either of them. There could be no improvement. He knew she wanted more, that she wanted to keep going, as if on a voyage, an epic: but he wanted it to stay the same, forever and ever; it was good, and it was safe.

They would go for a short walk right before she left for school: once around the block, or sometimes, if neither of them was saying anything, or they were sad—or if even only one of them was sad—then twice around the block.

Some mornings the car would not start, and she would have to take the brothers', or her parents', car. Someone would rescue her. It was a harbor. Her life was a harbor.

Kyle and Kale would be up after she had left, and Soozie and Heck, also—the sound of Soozie's hair drier, and Kale playing hard rock on the radio; Kyle, with no worries, no responsibilities, just his girlfriend, who would wait forever—Kyle sorting through the refrigerator, lifting his carton of milk out (a bicep drawn on it with a Magic Marker), and getting Kale's carton out for Kale (a heart with an arrow through it, and the word *Mom* inside the heart): the brothers standing around and drinking, swallowing the milk in long, cold gulps.

Heck, snapping and shutting, reopening and shutting his briefcase again and again, checking for papers: the only suit in the school, he dressed as if for church every day, and like Sukie, he distanced himself, in the mornings, from his family, from everything.

It was like going to war, like going on a hard and unhappy but challenging mission: and each day he had let himself get pulled away from love, from the harbor, until perhaps he did not even realize that he was leaving it; and each day he would come back, pretending he'd never left—smiles, and a father's interests, and a gin-and-tonic, a peck to Louella, mildness.

Watching A.C. and Sukie grow closer was, to Louella, like the pull of winter, or like giving birth. Always, she thought about the one she had lost. Twenty years later, she had been sent a replacement. She wanted to believe that. She believed it. She had not led a martyred life, but she had worked hard, and miracles happened. She wanted to believe it.

It was true, she realized. She could make it be true by wanting it to be true. It was happening.

She looked out her kitchen window, watched him sitting outside at the picnic table with his back to her, facing the garden, the late-season roses. Sun came through her kitchen window, and hummingbirds gradually came into the back yard, lured by the sweetness of the nectar she had put in the feeders.

Louella watched A.C. look around at the hummingbirds, watching them for the longest time, like a simple animal, like a brute.

Each morning, after the others had left, he would get up from the picnic table and come inside and tell her that he was going over to Vermont for a while—always, politely, he asked her if she needed anything, or if she cared to go with him, for the ride—always she refused, saying she had things to do (always, afterward, she wished she had said yes, wondered what it would be like, wondered what his old stone farmhouse looked like): but there were borders to be maintained, fences to remain standing, and she could not, would not, let go and say yes. She needed to stay around her own house, in case one of the children or Heck fell ill and had to come home.

So A.C. would lift the canoe over his head and walk through the neighborhood, out across the main road and down to the river, leaving her alone, leaving her waiting for everyone to come home.

What A.C. was working on in Vermont was a barn, for throwing the discus during the winter months. He had no more money left at all, not even a penny for gas, and he was ripping down old abandoned barns, saving even the nails from the old boards, and out in the woods, up on the side of the hill behind his farmhouse, he was making a long, narrow barn, more like a bowling alley than anything else.

He had measured, and it was 300 feet long. He climbed high into the trees to nail on the tall roof that would keep the snows out. There was not enough wood to build sides for the barn; mostly it was like a tent, a long, open-walled shed, to keep the snow from falling inside; he had built up the sides with stones about three feet high to keep the drifts from blowing in. It would be cold, but it would be free of snow.

He cut the trees down with an ax, to build the throwing

lane, and then cut them into lengths to be dragged away. He was building a strip of empty space in the heart of the woods, the wilderness; it ran for a hundred yards and then stopped.

He was keeping it a secret from the whole family, and was greatly pleased with his progress as the fall went on.

The air inside the throwing room felt purified, denser somehow. It had the special scents and odors of the woods. He burned all the stumps, leveled the ground with a shovel and hoe, and made a throwing ring out of river stones.

The rafters overhead reminded him of the church he'd gone to once with the Irons: the high ceiling, the beams, keeping the hard rains and snows out, protecting them, but also somehow distancing them from what it was they were after.

He would work on the barn all morning, and leave in time to get home and do his paper route, and still be back to the house before anyone else got there. Sometimes Louella would be out shopping, or doing other errands. He would sit at the picnic table and wait, not having thought about Sukie all day, but thinking about her now and listening for her car.

Thinking, I will do better today. I will go a little closer this evening. Not thinking of fears. Or anything.

There were still weekends to hold on to; and after throwing, on Friday afternoons—Soozie and Sukie watching, wearing their sweaters, now that it was cool—they would all go to a movie, and then out for pizza, and then, finally, back home for the late-night episode of *M*A*S*H*, Sukie unable to keep her eyes open by this time, sleeping with her head on A.C.'s shoulder, and everyone sprawled around the den like animals after a heavy feed, like lions gorged and napping.

Later in the month they built fires, and as Soozie sat by the fireplace and watched both the movie and her family, her red hair flashed as if lit from within. She watched them all as if she could learn from them, from all the ones who had gone before her, by watching: by being the youngest.

Soozie sat close to the fire, her arms around her knees, leaning forward and shivering sometimes, or just shuddering—a chill down her spine but nowhere else—and she watched Sukie and saw how tired she was.

They would all sleep that way then, straight through the night; sprawled about that one room of the house, a family: the real family, Patty staying over and sleeping on the rug, too, some nights, and Louella, coming in to make coffee on Saturday morning, would smile at them, at all of them, sometimes even nudging one of them with her foot. They had stopped putting the statues up at night, and the statues stayed where they were, covered by the canvas tarps, forgotten.

He could stay. She was so glad to have all of them. She couldn't imagine getting by without every one of them; she couldn't imagine what it would be like to lose even one now. He could stay.

"How was the movie?" she would ask.

Snow fell on the Hudson highlands, on the third of October, a Friday night. They were walking to the movie theater, all of them: A.C. and Sukie holding hands, Soozie running ahead of them. It was too early for snow, too soon.

The brothers were as full of spirit as they had been all year. It was as if they were all fourteen. They danced, did their discus spins in crowded places, ending their imaginary releases with wild whoops that drew some spectators and chased others away; all three of them whirling and twirling, leaping and whooping in the mall—Kale's and Kyle's spins still infinitely more polished and practiced than A.C.'s, but A.C.'s impressive also, nonetheless, if for nothing other than his great size and his own whoops (he pictured it being late spring still, or early summer, before he had even met them: back when he was still dancing with cows on his back)—and soon there was a large audience, clapping and cheering as if the brothers were Russian table dancers, giving them plenty of room, whistling and chanting, stamping their feet.

Sukie shrieked and hid her eyes with her hands, embarrassed, and Soozie blushed her hard crimson color, but was petrified, unable to move, and she watched them, as always, amazed. Sukie's fingers were digging into Soozie's arm; Sukie's wild shrieks—she was laughing, she was in a sort of ecstasy, a different place. Soozie smiled bravely through her embarrassment, and was happy for Sukie. It seemed wonderful to Soozie, it seemed thin and rare. Everyone around them in the mall kept clapping and stamping their feet, while outside, the first snow of autumn kept coming down.

A.C. was getting stronger, faster, was covering more ground on his paper route. He was giving the money from the route to Heck and Louella, and as he made more money, he tried to give that to them as well, but they wouldn't hear of it. So he bought things and gave them to Sukie.

He bought whatever he saw, if he happened to be thinking about her; a kitten. Bouquets of flowers, jewelry, an NFL football, a smoked turkey.

Magazine subscriptions, heads of lettuce, oil filters for her car, a shower cap, fishing lures, an ax, a nightgown, boxes of candy cigarettes, stationery.

She was flattered, excited and happy the first few times he brought something home—the kitten was the first thing—but soon became alarmed at the volume, at the almost frantic, determined wastefulness, and finally had to ask him to stop. "Please," she said. "Really." Then she had to explain to him what she really wanted, what really made her happy, and he was embarrassed, felt a fool, for not having realized it before; for having tried to substitute. It was like throwing from his hip rather than with the spin, he realized.

They went out in the canoe again, that Saturday night, out on Lake George. There was a full moon and it was a still night at first, still and cold, and the moon was so bright that they could see the shore, even sitting far out on the water; they could see each other's face, each other's eyes; it was like some

43

dream-lit daylight, hard and blue and silver, with the sound of waves lapping and splashing against the side of their small boat, and it was cold, but they undressed anyway, they wanted to get closer, as close as they could; they wanted to be all there was in the world, the only thing left.

He covered her with the blanket they had brought, later, and kept her warm with that and with himself: their arms and faces a bright white outside the blanket, lying down in the canoe on the water and looking up at the giant moon, the ragged sprawl of ugly craters seeming to scar its perfection— and drained from making love to her, he fell asleep, dreaming in the warmth of the blanket and the roll of the boat on the lake that he was still in her, that they were still loving, and that they always would be.

"You were smiling," she said when he woke around midnight. She'd been watching him all night: watching him, and holding him, sometimes pulling him so close to her and hugging so tightly that she was sure he'd wake up, but he had slept on, exhausted. "What were you smiling about?"

"You," he said sleepily, still not sure he wasn't dreaming. "I was thinking about you."

It was the right answer. She was so happy.

A Halloween dance, at Sukie's school, one weekend. Several girls had been raped after the dance last year, and most of the teachers' cars had had their tires slashed, their windshields broken and radio antennas snapped—a few fires had been set around the school and had scorched the walls. Sukie was chaperoning this year; she went up there with Kyle and Kale and A.C., and stayed with them the whole time.

It was the first any of the brothers had seen the inside of the place, and they saw that it was a hellhole: dingy, dark, musty, and full of bad feelings.

Foul graffiti, swastikas, broken bottles, and children without hope: all of this nestled in the beautiful dark mountains, by a rushing river with waterfalls, under a moonless sky of bright cold stars, stars so close that there could have been hope, *should* have been hope.

The brothers moved Sukie through the dance all night, dwarfing her like bodyguards, over 700 pounds of bulk and muscle—she was almost hidden whenever she was in their midst—and they wore short-sleeved shirts, though it was a cold night, and the young thugs and bullies were awed and did not try to reach out from the crowd and squeeze her breasts, as they sometimes did on dares, and even the male teachers, married and unmarried, treated her with respect rather than lust; and there was no vandalism in the parking lot; the four of them sat up in the bleachers and watched the dance and listened to the loud music until midnight, and were relieved when it was time to go home.

The students walking out to the parking lot, driving home, up into the mountains, in old rumbling race cars, a dozen pregnancies to occur before morning, perhaps, the mountains of lost hope, the mountains of anger—and the brothers and Sukie felt almost guilty, driving home to warmth and love; they rode in silence, thinking their own thoughts, back down into Glens Falls, whose lights they could see below, not twinkling as if with distance but shining steadily, a constant glow, because they were so close.

Geese, heading south, late in the year; stragglers. A.C. worked on his barn in the mild sunny days of November. He could feel snow coming, could feel it coming the way an animal can. The hair on his arms and legs was getting thicker, the way it had in Colorado in past falls. The barn reminded him of the one that had been out there in Colorado—the hay barn. That was where she had done it.

The throwing barn was almost finished. It was narrow. His throws would have to go straight. There could be no wildness or he would wreck the place he had built. He would teach himself to throw straight. The throws would not count if they did not fly straight.

He finished the barn in mid-November, as the big flakes were coming down, the second snow of the season, the snows which came and would not go away, not until the end of the season. He brought the brothers up to see it then, to show them how they could keep training together, how they could keep throwing all through the winter, even with snow banked all around them, and they were delighted.

"This is the best year of my life," Kale said unexpectedly.

A.C. bought a metal detector, and throws that did not travel perfectly straight—the barn was only thirty feet wide— they would go out searching for in the snow, listening for the quickening of pulse, the rapid signal that told them they were getting near. They were using old metal discs now, which flew farther in the cold air by two or three feet, and the brothers ate more than ever, trained harder.

There was a stone wall at the end of the barn, the 300-foot mark, stacked all the way to the rafters and chinked with mud and sand and grass. A.C. had lodged a discus in it once, had skipped a few of them against its base.

Three hundred feet was such a great distance. It had never been reached before. Three hundred feet was magical, un-imaginable; it required witchcraft, an alteration of reality.

It took the brothers and A.C. about fifty seconds to walk 300 feet—that was how far away it was. A minute away; and unobtainable, or almost.

There was that one-minute walk, and then also, beyond it, there was the length of their lives.

Sometimes the throws went too far off into the woods, and the discuses were lost for good; other times, they went too high and crashed through the rafters and up into the sky above, like violent cannonballs, like bats from hell, cruel iron, seeking to destroy, looking to hurt something.

"Forget it," Kyle would say gruffly whenever A.C. threw outside the barn; they'd hear the snapping, tearing sound of branches being broken, out in the woods, and then the whack!

of the discus striking a tree trunk. Kyle would already be reaching for another disc, though, handing it to him.

"Come on, come on, shake it off," he'd say. "Past history.
Over and done with. Throw again. Shake it off."

As the winter deepened, they set their goals harder
and farther. Kyle and Kale wanted to throw 221 feet; and A.C.
wanted to be able to throw 300 feet on any given throw, any
occasion: not just once in a blue moon.

And he wanted Sukie. He wanted things to stay the same
forever. He wanted to build fences, take care, protect. Sometimes, while everyone was at school, Louella would ride in the
canoe with him up to the barn, to watch him throw; she had
come over to his side, believed in him, and she did that.
Louella wanted to know about his past, but A.C. simply
wouldn't tell her. He now believed that he had had none.

A.C. would build a little fire for Louella in the barn, and
she would sit on a stump and sip coffee and watch him as he
threw. His spin was getting better. It was an imitation of her
sons', she could tell: but it was starting, finally, to get some
fluidity to it, some life, some creativity.

The brothers had built a harness for A.C., which they
attached with ropes to a pulley up on a beam in the rafters, a
harness such as the ones gymnasts use; and sometimes, to help
smooth out his spin, they'd put him in the harness and walk
him through the motions, lifting him off the ground at the
appropriate times, Kyle pulling him up and down at the right
moments, while Kale, pushing from behind, moved him forward across the little throwing ring, showing him when to
accelerate, when to pause, when to stop and when not to.

Like a puppet, seemingly all tangled up in the ropes, being
controlled from above, he'd move across the throwing ring in
these practice spins, being pulled and pushed, chasing 300
feet; chasing that minute's walk.

Louella enjoyed watching him work, watching him train.
His clumsiness did not worry her, because, she could tell, he

was working at it and overcoming it. She was even able to smile, sometimes, when the discus soared up through the rafters, letting a sprinkle of snow pour down into the barn from above, yet another hole punched through the roof, one more hole of many, the snow sifting down like a fine, magical powder that would somehow make him stronger next time.

They were alarming, those wild throws, but she found herself trusting him. And secretly, too, she liked the wild throws: she was fascinated by the strength and force behind them, the utter lack of control. It was like standing at the edge of a volcano, looking down. She would move a little closer to the fire and watch. She was fifty-eight, and was seeing things she'd never seen before, feeling things she'd never felt. Life was still a mystery. He had made her daughter happy again, brought her out of last year's sadness-for-no-reason.

"Keep your head back," Louella would caution whenever she saw that his form was too terribly off. She knew enough about it to tell how it was different from her own sons', when it was wrong. Or: "Keep your feet spread, your feet were too close together."

Everyone helping him. And he helped them.

The whole family came for Thanksgiving: cousins and moved-away aunts and little babies and uncles, nieces. Everything flowed; he was a fit; it was as if he'd always been there, and he always had been. Passing the turkey, telling jokes, teasing Soozie about a boyfriend; laughter, and warmth, inside the big house.

The roads iced over; the sound of studded snow tires outside, and of chains clanking. Football all day on television, and more pie, more cider, the brothers the largest men in town. Thanksgiving passed, and they were on into December, the Christmas season, with old black-and-white movies on television late at night and Sukie home from school on vacation, everyone home, and he was firmly into their center, her center, everyone's; it would be the place and time where he could do the most damage; it was the time to do it, if it were to happen, he was into the spin of love and asked her to marry him, and did not hurt her, did not hurt anyone.

"Yes," she said, laughing, remembering last year's sadness and the crazy, utter lost hope of it, never dreaming or knowing that he had been out there, moving toward her like an object already thrown, flying a great distance, and somewhat out-of-bounds, but thrown with force and effort. There was a danger in the distance, but also an excitement, and in her dreams, in the nights preceding the wedding, she saw images of summer, June coming around again; she and her mother were out in a large field, with cattle grazing out near the trees, and in the field there were great stones and boulders, fieldstones left over from another age, a time of glaciers and ice, perhaps, or of great floods.

And in the dreams, she and her mother were leaning into the boulders, rolling them, moving them out of the field, making the field pure and green. They were building a stone wall out of the boulders, all around the field, and some of the boulders were too large to move; Sukie would grit her teeth and push harder, straining, trying to move them all out of the field. Then she would wake up and be by his side, by his warmth, and would realize that she had been pushing against him, trying to push him out of bed, but that it could not be done, and she'd laugh and put her arms around as much of him as she could, and bury her face in him, and then would get up after a while, unable to sleep.

She'd dress and put on her snow boots and go out into the garage and pick up and hold one of the discuses, holding it with both hands, feeling the worn smoothness of it, the coldness, and also the magic of it—magic, Sukie believed, because he had touched it—and then, certain that no one was watching, that no one could ever find out, she would go into the front yard, dressed like an Eskimo, and under the blue cast of the streetlight she'd crouch and then whirl, spinning around and around, and throw the discus as far as she could, in whatever direction it happened to go; and she'd shout, almost roar, and watch it disappear into the soft new snow; jumping up and down afterward, sometimes, when she threw really well and was pleased with her throw.

Then she would wade out through the new and falling snow to where she had seen the discus disappear, and would dig for it with her hands, kneeling down, searching for it all the rest of the night sometimes; but always finding it, and never panicking, never worrying that one time she might not find it: because it was always in her yard, and A.C. was in her bed, sleeping; and under the snow, then, she'd find it, find it like a lost child, and carry it back into the garage, slip it back into the box with the others, and she'd be able to sleep then, cold but growing warm again in bed with him; warm with life, warm with hope, and with the outline of danger somewhere out there, far enough away to define the warmth, far enough away not to be a threat.

Not when she was so close to hope. Not when she was almost reaching it, knocking right at its door, pitching stones against its base and dreaming of summer, of her mother, and of stone fences, barns, and things built by hand.

She had never been so excited before, and she told herself it was worth the risk, worth any risk.

In the spring, then, before the wedding, after the snows melted and the river began to warm—the river in which the brothers had first seen him swimming—A.C. began to train that way again, only training with Sukie that year, rather than with the brothers, because he had made his choice and it was the direction to go now.

A.C. would wear a wet suit, because the water was still too cold, and flippers; and he'd fasten a rope and harness around his chest and tie the other end of it to the bumper of her car, before leaping into the river from a high rock, into the rapids, and being washed through them, downstream.

Then he would try to swim upriver, against the force of nature, against the water's power; and he'd do it again and again, until his shoulders were screaming, until he was too

tired to even lift his head, and was nearly drowning; and Sukie
would leap in the car then and start it up, and ease up the hill,
pulling him, like a limp wet rag, up through the rapids,
through the waves he'd been fighting, and on farther up the
river, until he was in the stone-bottomed shallows, and she'd
park the car, set the emergency brake, and jump out and run
back down to get him.

Like a fireman, she'd pull him the rest of the way out of
the river, splashing knee-deep in the water, helping him up,
putting his arm around her tiny shoulders; and somehow
they'd stagger up into the rocks and trees along the shore; and
like a drowned man, or a beached whale, saved, he'd lie on his
back and gasp, looking up at the sky and the tops of trees, and
smelling the scent of pines, of warming sun.

They would lie in the sun, drenched, exhausted, until their
clothes were almost dry, and then they would back the car
down and do it again.

He liked being saved. She liked saving him. It was the only
way it worked. He needed her. She knew he wouldn't leave. He
was too close to being saved. She was the only one who could
do it. He had been lost twice—once at birth, and then again,
in Colorado. She knew he probably was her brother, or had
been, at one time: but she was the only one who could save
him, and she would do whatever it took. Closer and closer
she'd pull him, reeling in the wet rope, dragging him up on
shore; bending over and kissing his wet lips until his eyes
fluttered, bringing him back to life, every time. Q

Sūcan

The pulling suck sounds have begun. The still-sporadic, rhythmless pulling, the steep lunar sucking that will make the earth's surface as slick as hair oil, make the air on severance day pungent and voluptuous, salt-sprayed, so rubbery. People sense "something in the air," but what? When? Is this IT? we say. Here in lovely Croix de Bouquets, where the smoke drifts in acrid plumes and the taste in the air is of sugar burning and raw meat waiting, where diamonds flash in the parks and the blue-eyed camels left over from the days of the circus traverse the thoroughfares, we speak with a certain detachment of disaster approaching. Oh yes, we say. Rupture, and famine, flood, drought, the bottom falling out, the top falling in, always something. But here, beneath a tropical sky, the saying also goes that the only certain changes are those of the weather.

Would that we were more given to concentration, less caught up in life, or even better informed, but the newspaper only publishes gossip and the gossip is always based on fantasy. What to do but consider the landscape, suck a finger and hold it to the sky, check the direction of the wind, peer from the verandah into the heart of the city, where the answers surely lie. There where the mass slaughtering of mourning doves has taken place, where the beggars have vanished. But where, for the moment, the hour is almost serene.

At midday on the floor of the palace aviary the President-General sits plucking the presidential goose. His left foot rests in the lap of his manicurist, his huge head in the sling that swoops down from the cherry picker. What kind of life is this? Orgasm-gold nail polish on the toes. Slender fingers pulling feathers from the golden rump, filling the rose-colored carpetbag with down, rubbing his pockmarked cheeks and ears through the muslin of the sling. The gecko tongue running out and in, rubbing against swollen lips; the amazing tongue that lets the owner hang from high places, the dangerous hairs adhering to the surface of ceiling wood or to the smoked glass of an antique mirror.

That sling could be slashed. The tongue could be severed. Then goose down would billow up and descend to rest on a sticky foot, a painted toe. In the branches high above, the birds would burst into song.

The woman climbing from the taxi in front of Sammy's wants to know what has become of the beggars.

Nobody knows. Or nobody speaks. The beggars have been carted off, at some hour before dawn. Driven into the country-side and let loose like mice. Or maybe buried in quicklime on Île-à-Vache. Only threads in the gutters now and pieces of sandal made of tire treads.

The woman closing the door to the taxi in front of Sammy's says, "Anyway, clean streets. Let us not dwell on the mechanics of how. Think of what was. The hands clutching at the hem, the stumps thrust through the ironwork. The fetidness of it all. And the hopelessness. They followed you right up the drive, you know. Right into the pool."

The woman has just come from a wedding, and in her pocketbook there rests a whole ham, so pink and greasy and succulent and clove-ridden, there in the comforting depths of the white cotton with eyelet borders, beside the gold compact and ten one-hundred-dollar bills, each one as soft and powdery as a powdered cheek, as filthy as a human hand. The woman has removed the ham from the buffet table at the reception, which is considered acceptable behavior here: snatching, hoarding, perhaps devouring.

Acts for which there are no reasonable explanations.

There is an intensification of street noise these days. The casual crackle of gunshot, sirens at midday, the revving up of the motorcycle escort, the wa-wa-wa-ing of the Mercedeses as they careen through narrow streets. And again and again, on balconies, in high-ceilinged rooms beneath the slow-turning ceiling fans, the suggestion of a passionate encounter. The invitation to desire. Fingers searching here and there in an open mouth.

All very good for the hotel business.

"Do we eat unwashed?" the photographer asks. He is lying beside the hotel pool, having a pedicure, popping tetracycline tablets to speed up the tanning process. His body is the orange color of throat medicine and medicated Band-Aids.

"Do we chance the unboiled?"

"Why has the river trip been canceled?"

"Dahling," the actress tucked into the inner tube says. "Dahling. Oh, dahling, here I am paddling along the frolicsome edge of the Sea of Galilee and I can only tell you that of course I think your Jesus was a wild success. I think he was a divine leader. And attractive. But, you know, just a person. And don't look, but I think your toe has been severed from its station on your foot."

"Oh my God," the photographer says, "oh, my God, an open wound. *Here*?"

The manicurist, flustered, frightened, without anything close at hand to calm the bleeding, looks to her husband the masseur, down at the far end of the pool, where he bends over Lady Ordsmore and Brann's emaciated body; staring, lost, unhelpful. The manicurist pulls the photographer's foot into the pool and the water quivers.

The pulling sounds and the feeling of sucking. Get it? We are talking about Birth or Death, or the desecration of the land. Instructions for sex or for downing a poached egg. Or, more likely, the severing of the city from the continent. The sucking up of the steamy streets and dry riverbeds and squatters' boxes. And the many domes of the sea-foam candy palace right into the earth's atmosphere, out of sight.

A *How To* list circulates. "Here's the pitch," the ex-Minister of Culture says over noontime rum and lime. The man stands as though on stage, leaning into an imaginary wind, playfully tweaking the good pearls that droop from his pet borzoi's thready neck, speaking as though we were deaf. "Regarding massive uproot, final suck-up, figure:

> Binding, swaddling, pegging beepers, winching.
> Hoving, marking lift notches, melting, installing.
> Piping funnels, floating bobbers, nutting.
> Attachment of umph risers and canopy tweeters.
> Wool blowers, layettes, cream, tucking the wump.
> Finally wooshes and dog sleds."

The Minister bows and drags the dog to the railing.

A woman says, "Am I missing something?"

"Is there time for a bath?" someone inquires from the street. "Time for a bath?"

It would appear that decisions made at some point in the past, for reasons no longer remembered, by people no longer interested or even alive, demand answers that do not appear to be forthcoming. It is the natural state of affairs in a port town where people have been driven in upon themselves and tend to exhibit a certain theatrical quality, an inventiveness, the playwright's gift for making up the truth.

Meanwhile, the Richy Riches have arrived. This team of mulatto and albino terrors has zoomed in without prior announcement, and already an elaborate show takes place within the ring of limousines. There are no tickets, but people living in high places are able to look onto the flea circus, the last on earth, so far as we know, the only other of note having been attended by a number of us at the Tivoli Gardens in Copenhagen in 1959 and that one lacking the aerial act with the couple pushing the baby buggy. There is also the high dive into the plastic pool, whose collapsible sides give way as the diver hits the water, lending the impression of a miracle. The diver appears to have taken off from the top of the four-story fire ladder and landed not in twelve inches of water but on the circle of concrete.

"Not dead," people cry as the seventy-five-year-old albino daredevil with the puffed chest and froggy body stands and bows and accepts flowers and coins to put into the bathing cap he carries in his wet hands.

"What's it like?" we cry. And of course, "Why? Why?"

There is also Madame de Capitata and the man with the skin of a snake, but these acts are not as stunning. After the show de Capitata can be seen yawning and sipping her decaffeinated tea from the tailgate of her Persian automobile, and the snake man is known to be a problem at small balls.

"Remember," Big Head announces on the afternoon news, "without change there is no news, and there is no news."

The port captain, who has been putting notes into bottles, reports his returns. A grain of sand, a mosquito, and a cigarette with lipstick smeared across the tip. Then a bottle containing a pair of ships made of cement.

Because the pulling sounds we hear are in many ways familiar, they are, perhaps, deceptively reassuring. The sounds could be no more than the echoes of anchor ropes straining in a night wind, or of journeys taken. Of straps that flap against a leather carryall, or the ripping of canvas seams to relieve the pressure of too much forced into a space. Of zippers ripping. Or the wheezing syncopation of bedsprings, so that the language of disaster enveloping us could also be the language of love in the night, when people place their hands in front of their eyes and convince themselves that not a single moving finger can be seen, or love as the light is beginning, when the fishing boats are already moving from the lagoon, into the harbor, and out toward the open sea, the boats steered in wandering patterns, like moths across the water, by lantern light with the battered outboard motors running, the sun behind the mountains, not yet touching the bare feet braced against the gunwales, while lovers turning in their beds strike matches to mark the hour, and fall back, each one, once more, into a slumber full of the other.

We lie in our hammock, sometime after dawn, wrapped in felt to keep off the night chill, and feel the sucking. Feel something nudging us and drawing us on. The reminder of what we were and of what we will surely become, of how we started out and how we will certainly end our days.

Once, wrinkled pink crones who washed ashore and searched with budding lips offered up our toothless nibbles at the beachheads, little blistered-mouth persons who wandered on the soft landscape, feeling our way across the moony terrain of a mother. The arrival was everything in those days, the journey touched with desperation.

In the present, the sucking sounds come as mood music, while our bellies slip against each other and our tongues are bound in rich glossal pleasures, but there is also the promise of life being drawn out of us, of death sūcan us into eternity. And we do not want to be there, in Dark Eternity.

Phil Pleets does not concern himself with Dark Eternity. Bellies in the mud, wet backsides walloping against porcelain tubs, hot-lady jazz, the satisfying wump of teeth being separated from the plaster with which he makes the impressions—these are Phil Pleets's concerns. Suck, suck, Pleets's own empty belly growls, and his patient feels her teeth sink into the pink ooze and hears Phil Pleets getting ready for his weekend in the countryside, switching to weekend talk now, saying, "I'm hearin primal, baby. Hang on to the jaw. I'm givin pull."

Pleets has dozens of gleaming pastel jaws, all rigid and crooked and ape-like, grinning down from the dusty glass shelf beside the mural of the Eiffel Tower and the rattling papery pods of the Bois Noir tree. Pleets is a musician as well as a dentist and a drug addict, having weaned himself from the trumpet's kiss of laughing gas only to find himself drawn with dancing feet of the bridegroom to the cocktail injections he administers to victims of abscess and impacted wisdom teeth, chanting as he prepares both himself and the patient "a little cocktail here, a little cocktail there, ha ha ha ha, ha ha, and we are goners all!"

Pleets approaches every riff with head stuffed into a hat that features a battery-operated light on the visor. Bending over his patient now, his sweet victim, wrenching the trough of hardening ooze from her sweet mouth, for which Pleets promises the charm of a new arrangement—moving the little birds all a half inch to the left, or pulling the wisdom tooth and seeing what happens, seeing nature herself start to monkey around in there—Pleets travels by the light of his lantern and warbles and wrenches, and the patient feels the fragile jaw cracking, only a hairline fracture, but the pain makes her dizzy, makes her cry out, "Pleets."

And Pleets nods, he knows, he has broken many a jaw in the service of law and order; he has just the thing, the famous cocktail, and songs from the forties, a jab for you and a jab for me, love, and a bit of wire, no more suckin for this one, another jab, why not, and the wounded one sees the sky darken while Phil Pleets hums. Patching and humming, Pleets gazes in amazement at the blood on his hands, puts the water on to boil for the coffee, grinds the beans, pours, blows the grounds down, and they sit and sip, in a common twilight, side by side, swinging their legs from the edge of the campaign bed, bruising their lips on the tin cups, emerging slowly from the mist, Pleets rising to search for ice to pack against the saddened jaw, but there is only a quart of Boodles in that refrigerator, so it will be black eyes tonight, and swollen cheeks, and life through a straw for one of them, while out there along the harbor the winches continue to turn.

Still, we insist upon a certain stateliness. The blue-eyed camels continue to traverse the thoroughfares. The cafés continue to do a record business. The film festival opens and posts the notice that the weekend showing of *The Royal Road to*

Romance has sold out. The deliveries of bottled water brought in from Japan to fill the empty riverbed are abruptly canceled, but the brown river bottom is lined with white stones, and a blue ribbon is laid to show the course of what might have been. The ribbon blows along, lending delight and color as well as opportunities for employment and distraction. An aluminum boat is placed on the ribbon, holding within its blazing-hot confines four aluminum seats covered with cushions to be used in case of someone flipping out of the boat, or the boat springing a leak, or a man batting a woman with an oar and the woman being flung afar and starting to drown immediately, as in a story of crime and love gone wrong, or a story of natural disaster. Sure. A tropical cyclonic burst coming up from wherever, spiraling along and spewing gale-force winds and velocitous and torrential rains, twirling this way and that, pausing just long enough to avoid beating the warning signals; the blood-orange clouds, the long sea swells, the slick, unbroken, fishy wave, the charmed sailors seated on the steaming cushions looking up at the ominous eye of the storm, thinking, Here it comes, batten down, hang onto your hat, or, not knowing, thinking, Divine calm weather, no? People forget that the riverbed is empty, that the missing water was not, in any case, sea water.

"Perhaps the water will return," the ex-debutante murmurs to the gangster. "In our country we have miracle mornings. We take an interest in food. We toot our horns."

The gangster has slipped out of his riding boots and drawstring pajamas. He tightens his shoulder holster. He props his body on the downy pillows. His hands coddle the small revolver. His tongue probes the chilled air.

"I do what I have to do," the gangster says. "I live in the present. I am what I am."

"Oh hey," the woman says as the doors to the bedroom open. "What is this? Hey. Where are my gloves?"

The baptism takes place on a Saturday. The guests gather

in the gazebo at the end of the pier. Then, dazzle dazzle dazzle, darling. Into the pale pajama blue of a high-noon springtime sea, the infant goes, down through layers of sunlight and plankton, past parrot fish, butterfish, milk rays, mother heads with calm sleep eyes, and the tongues reaching, dangling, offering, past coral villages from which the toes of sailors protrude in such a way as to express both homesickness and repose, past the sleeping white sharks and muscles of fathers undulating in the currents of caves.

Down.

The infant has slipped from the arms of the godfather, who was gazing at something, trying to remember the child's name, trying to remember his own name, trying to remember why they are here, to what purpose? is there to be cake and champagne? is he expected to give a toast? He cannot remember the words to any songs.

"Good show," a man shouts.

"Perfect stroke."

"Bravo!"

Champagne is opened.

"To life. To something."

"Three cheers for Bill. For Polly."

"What is the name of the fabulous swimmer?"

Even the parents are amazed. The child is a natural, though an elevator operator suggests that something is amiss.

Then a banker makes a throat-slicing motion with the side of his hand. "Six minutes and you've had it," the man reports. "Karroom. Yazoo." The banker sucks in with his tongue, then blows out violently, with his tongue pressed against his teeth.

"He's a bit much," a woman says.

The banker gives the back-of-the-hand motion to the woman, who faints. Or worse. Probably worse, nothing is certain. The infant, out of sight, very nearly out of mind, is zipping along nicely, through the layers of sea life, in the direction of one of the world's great divers and underwater lovers, the husband of five, the father of five times five, or more, more than anyone can count, one man of the sea named Oliverio de Ponce, who lies musing on the sandy white awning of a partly submerged touring car, waiting for his mistress, eyeing the approach of the golden object, this fishlike child, this chortling mammal, trailing the white nightgown.

"O wondrous one!" Oliverio de Ponce whispers, opening his arms and causing bubbles to gush.

"To longevity, then!" goes the cry on the pier.

"To aquatics!"

At that moment, the heavens expanded and sucked us up, easily, into a billowing and transparent skinlike form, carrying us and our port city far and fast and in near-silence, except for the many screams and shouts of those all around, and I thought, How can this be happening? The prophecy of this moment in time was only a way of describing the rhythms of life, a figure of speech, you see, in the manner of poets and soothsayers. It was not expected. Then, looking down, I saw the children coming up from the sea, crossing the shallows, converging upon the shore, staggering and stumbling, hundreds upon thousands of children slipping and reaching and spreading out, moving across the black beaches where the surf ran yellow, across the tidal pools and marsh grasses, toward places we would never dream of, and I whispered, not realizing that my whisper was a shout, saying that we ought to have proceeded differently, with extreme care and with compassion, and patience, and wonder, yes, wonder, a sense of wonder, and awe, and ceremony, and mystery.

Oh, shut up! one nearest me cried, can you not see we are going to the dogs? Can you not see it is over? and I nodded, and raised my hands, and placed them over my face, and over my eyes, for it was turning dark and my wagging fool's tongue would not be useful here. Q

A Dish of Radishes

This is the bitter truth, thought Milkowsky. He stared at the red radish on his chipped white plate. A stinging had begun in his stomach only a few moments before as he sorted the herring away from the tomatoes in the salad bowl.

The cafeteria was called The New Yorker. It was an all-night affair on the avenue named Blue Hill, which ran out of Boston toward that eminence to the south and dragged the Jews along with it through Roxbury, Dorchester, and Mattapan. Now few Jews are there. Business is charcoal—burned-out stores and fried chicken. The New Yorker, when it first opened, must have suggested to the Boston Yiddish palate sophisticated taste. In its last days, the restaurant was home to a despair that had been pickling since the days of King Nebuchadnezzar and the heartburn of overlays—German, Polish, and Russian cuisine. It was possible to eat a meal at three in the morning, kishke, kasha, and varnitchkes, a plate of potato latkes. That's what Milkowsky was doing. It meant that he had slipped down the back stairs through the kitchen door of his third-floor apartment on Wales Street.

Snoring in the back bedroom were Milkowsky's wife, Sara Dvayrah, and the baby, while in the dining room, now a second bedroom, his daughters, Esther and Malkeh, were, he was sure, wetting the beds.

Heavy sleepers, they were left by Jerry Milkowsky as unconscious of his departure as creatures wedded to time in an enchanted castle. The stairs creaked and the linoleum cracked under his cautious tread toward the street below, but the Bernsteins on the second floor, and the Cohens on the first, slept with the concentration of the just, searching in dreams for the answers to riddles of dry goods, supply and demand, the mysteries of textiles and the night.

What was Milkowsky's red-and-white slice? His eyes watered as The New Yorker, its countermen with bleared eyes, its customers—Jewish bookies, Irish prostitutes, truck drivers, cabbies, night-shift workers—rolled toward the pink iris of dawn. The sun would streak on the faces of the breakfast tribe, a people as different from The New Yorker's inhabitants at three in the morning as the Hittites from the children of Nippur. At five, the crowd was early risers, mainly salesmen out to beat the competition on the road to Peterborough, Concord in New Hampshire, Springfield, Bangor, up wolfing down eggs, bagels, cream cheese, whitefish. Milkowsky sat among insomniacs, foot-draggers, confidence men, girls whose dresses and seams were cut too deep, the empty shadows, too tight, too short, all those who, by choice, avoid the sharp light of morning, its optimistic but merciless definition.

Milkowsky had lost his job. It wasn't worth having, he had insisted to his wife as she began to cry and tear at her blouse, the children running to her skirts from the corners of the room. A salesman in a lamp store, Milkowsky had wandered for over a year between bronze and brass stems, but in the last few months the glass and crystal mantles he knocked over came to more than his salary. The owner, his wife's cousin, had to ask Milkowsky to close the door of the store in Roxbury behind him. The proprietor was sad. To his surprise, Milkowsky was a good salesman, with a knack of moving expensive merchandise, getting the poorest customers to spend beyond the budget penciled on the slips in their pockets. "What room are you lighting?" That's how the young man began. It was so innocent, so technical, it caught off guard the guy or family who had come in the door to poke around. The owner never did it that way. The idea of a sales pitch for lamps seemed impossible.

"How much do you want to spend?" the owner had begun, for thirty-five years now, wholesale or retail. Then the proprietor had taken the customers carefully, lamp by lamp, to everything in that price range and let them make up their own minds. There were too many lamps, too many mind changes, too many styles. Give them a good price, tell them to check it down the Avenue, and if the people were swaying back and forth dangerously, knock off ten percent and pull out a pad of sales slips to steady them.

Milkowsky's second question was "What kind of light do you like in the house?"

"A nice light," his wife's cousin would have answered.

Milkowsky started in with adjectives before the customer could open his mouth. "Hazy? Theatrical?" Words that weren't in the brochures. "You want an inquisitive probing trajectory coming down on the table?" the young man shot out. "Or do you want something subdued, modest, background light? What do you want to do in the kitchen? Play pinochle, have your children study, use it as a dining room, have it double as a pantry? You want to set it up so as to switch functions, or do you want an all-purpose unitary source?"

The owner was ready to rush out and hit the kid with a stick the first time, but the customer bought. It gave the proprietor chills: something dirty going on in the shadows of his business. He heard the line slip out of his salesman before closing one night—"What's your fantasy?"

It worked, though, for nine or ten months, and just when, despite his own distaste for these methods (even the electricians started coming up to Milkowsky with their orders), the owner was thinking of teaching the kid bookkeeping and was holding out a promise of a small share in the business profits, Milkowsky started banging into lamps. His wife's cousin heard the globes shatter and, after a day or two, discovered him, deliberately shutting his eyes, lunging this way and that at odd moments between sales. After a month and a half, it didn't add up anymore and talking to Milkowsky didn't do anything either: all sorts of crazy excuses: the lamps stacked the wrong way, slippery floors. The owner told Milkowsky to take a vacation. "I'll call you in a few weeks," he mumbled, blinking into his brightest illuminations, as the kid went out the door.

Milkowsky didn't go home. He went to The New Yorker and sat until his father, who poked his head in after the eight o'clock service at the local synagogue, found him there in the morning, reading a paper.

Milkowsky's father was retired. He had a heart condition. A tiny pension from the needle trade gave him just enough to live on. Milkowsky's mother was in the mental institution behind an iron fence just a few streets away. Neither Milkowsky nor his father ever knew when they might see her on the street, lipstick zigzagging down her chin, rouge and powder on her forehead: the patients were often allowed to wander for a few hours in the afternoon in the direction of the Avenue.

Very few words passed between Milkowsky and his father. The latter waited by the door of The New Yorker. The food was unclean according to strict Orthodox law, and the older man had become scrupulous about keeping kosher in the years since his retirement. Finally, the son got up, and the two of them walked toward the steep descent of Wales Street. The father started up the stairs before the son, knocking softly on the door. Sara Dvayrah opened it. Milkowsky saw from his wife's face that she had called his father during the night and that nothing would be said until he had had a cup of tea at their table, had patted the heads of the three children, and, having said two or three words to the baby, had gotten to his feet, thanked Sara Dvayrah, and closed the door behind him.

The sun was already low in the sky when Milkowsky awoke, his cheek creased against the hard pillows of the couch. The baby was hitting his face as he lifted it. The force of the blow was stronger than Milkowsky imagined a toddler could manage. Her sharp fingernails stung. With his eyes half open, he pushed the tiny hand away.

A shadow loomed over the child, who had begun to cry. Sara Dvayrah looked down, her scornful mouth twisted in an accusation: Milkowsky was beating the baby! The only way to escape an argument that would go on and on for days—Sara Dvayrah hooking him and dragging him through her frustration, reeling him in on an endless line, knotted from every night he had avoided her bed, from every rumor she had heard of a girl friend whose husband had become successful, bought a new car or house, taken a vacation—was to be still. The baby returned to the couch, battered him with her miniscule fists, but the father had turned his face into the pillows and the child gave up after a few moments of assaulting a dead fish.

For the rest of the afternoon, Milkowsky dozed in the middle of his household's noises, pulling the afghan down from the top of the couch back to cover himself. From under the pillow, he heard his wife stamp away. Later the door slammed, and his older daughters skipped into the house, shouting, then whispering, tiptoeing. The baby kept coming up to the couch to pummel the back of the figure draped in a blanket. Once, she even scrambled up and bit. Milkowsky didn't shiver. The volume subsided. Forks and knives were scraping plates. "Are you eating?" Milkowsky ignored the impersonal bark. An overturned dish cracking was the sole punctuation. Daylight in the room had faded, and the faraway fluorescent ring of the kitchen left his couch in relative darkness.

Damp diapers and unwashed underwear made the four rooms a pismire. Sara Dvayrah—who in adolescence had seemed like a female animal, erotic, generous—slapped around the house in lopsided slippers, fat hanging in loops from her belly button. In the mirror, Milkowsky's hair thinned. The two older daughters whined like police whistles. He could not respond to tugs of affection at his pants. He pushed the girls away, and their mother led them in angry shuffles around him. In the past few weeks, Milkowsky had stayed home from work three, four days, a headache fastened like a loop of thorns tightening around his scalp. Milkowsky slept through the mornings, dragged himself between bathroom and living-room couch, in the afternoon burying himself in newspapers, college texts ranged in the single bookcase, battered copies of Nietzsche, on whom he had written a thesis, not accepted. Because of the baby, a six o'clock riser, Sara Dvayrah went to bed early and Milkowsky was able to slip out around ten.

The white flesh of the radish, firm but oozing its sting-ing colorless spice out of a scarlet jacket, parted under Mil-kowsky's knife. It was black beyond the windows of The New Yorker. In the absence of daylight, anything could happen. Between the balconies of the Avenue, the hollows swelled in pinned-up sheets, wrung out to dry. Milkowsky's eyes watered: the sharp vegetable under his nose. He let go, fell, sliding down a rooftop into the street, or from the clothesline strung from the back porch of his third-story apartment to a dead oak at a fence line. Jerry began to chew the radish half, wincing, when he caught sight of a girl at the next table.

She was sitting in the short skirt of the skating rink, but looked older than the teenage patrons of the roller-ball hall, tough girls from the blue-collar neighborhoods beyond the Jewish streets. Irish, Polish, Ukrainian, a few Italian. They came by trolley or bus, sometimes in the back of a beat-up car, to the evening sessions at the skating rink across the Avenue and a street or two down from the restaurant. The girl Mil-kowsky saw, who now stared back at him, was sitting in a group of taxi drivers, regulars at The New Yorker. Through the mist in Milkowsky's eyes, he could make out her very white skin, her straight blond hair carefully curled into ringlets that fell over her neck. Milkowsky could smell her perfume and couldn't stop staring. When the girl didn't break off looking across at him, after ten, fifteen seconds, Milkowsky rose shakily and took a few steps toward her table. "Do you mind?" he said. One of the cabbies, a man with a horse's face, creased in blue shad-ows, started to wave Milkowsky off, a counter fly, but another fellow opened his heavy-lidded eyes and, shifting the three hundred pounds he had squeezed under the table of the corner booth, breathed out hoarsely, "Sit down, sit down."

This was Meyer Landau. A CPA without a license, Landau had gone to Harvard and later to a federal penitentiary. He dressed in the black suit of a religious Jew, and the fringes of a short tallis came out of the explosion of his belt, shirt, and pants. In his vest pocket there was a Phi Beta Kappa key, and at times Landau wound its gold chain around the fingers of his left hand and drummed on the table. He didn't eat in The New Yorker but sat there giving advice, tips. The seventy-year-old busboy used to come by Landau's seat for them, then the relief, a kid with pimples who had dropped out of junior high. Landau liked to talk about philosophy, citing medieval rabbis, Aristotle, Platonists, Neo-Platonists, pelting the table where Milkowsky first sat with quotes as the teenagers at his elbow spat watermelon seeds from oversized slices onto a racetrack of paper napkins. The Harvard CPA had eaten himself into obesity, but the corners of his mouth, his small, flat, wrinkled nose, held the attention of girls and made Meyer welcome at the chairs of pimps and high-school delinquents.

"Thanks," said Milkowsky, coming closer toward Landau and the drivers.

The girl kept her blue eyes fixed on Milkowsky. His hands rattled the last radish off the salad plate, transferring it along with a coffee cup to the large table where Landau and the men sat with the blonde. She was at the open end of the horseshoe of people around the circular table. Milkowsky snuggled in, feeling the current run from bare legs to him under his worn baggy gray pants.

"This is Betty Daugherty," Landau called out, cutting across the banter of the pool sharks opposite her, as one of them tried to draw her back into the teasing of the taxi drivers.

"I'm Jerry," he said, looking into the girl's eyes.

"Jerry what?" She returned his sharp stare.

"Milkowsky."

"Hi, Jerry," she said.

The way the girl opened her mouth, her tongue flickering at him, gave Milkowsky heart to leap across the space. "What's your philosophy?"

"What's yours?" Betty asked.

"Myself." Milkowsky was staring at her, but he could feel it was dangerous.

"Is that philosophy?" she said, as if amused.

"That's what it comes down to," he retorted.

The girl's eyes narrowed, and for a second Milkowsky lost sight of the blue light. "Why? Wh . . . what did you think it was?" he stammered. They had managed to shut out the rest of the table. Landau was leading off in a monologue, provoking enough laughter to keep the taxi drivers from leaning in.

"Something better." Her eyes opened for a moment.

"Not me sitting at two in the morning on the Avenue, eating pickles, but me as *idea*," Milkowsky said slowly, ready to look away if she answered with a wisecrack.

"What kind of idea?" Betty asked him, looking serious.

"An idea of something better," the young man said, not sure he understood his own remark.

"What do you do?" she asked.

"Nothing. Exist. And you?" he responded, beginning to think Betty was smarter than she looked.

"The same," she countered.

"We must be the same person." Milkowsky said it and stared at her full in the face.

Instead of letting her lip curl up in amusement, Betty looked at him. Milkowsky took in her whole figure, the breasts filling out her green wool sweater. He wanted to put his hands in their shadows where they stretched the cable of the knit, grip the outline of her broad shoulders, the long line of her calves—what he could see under the table. Wanting to come up against her—lips, belly, legs—was so strong that Mil-

69

kowsky, dizzily breathing a harsh perfume like burning leaves, almost didn't hear her whisper, "I would like that."

"Why?" It slipped out of him like a wisecrack. Betty didn't answer. She half-turned back to the table.

A tremor like dry ice ran between Milkowsky's legs. He leaned forward and, not knowing what he meant, said, "Even when the mouth lies, the way it looks still tells the truth."

Betty Daugherty swung back. How blue her eyes were, a faint pink lipstick, the suggestion of a few freckles in her white complexion, as she scanned Milkowsky's face. She drew closer and put her nose almost next to his. They watched each other, and then she laughed, making him smile too. "That's very good," Betty said. "Did you think of that?"

"No, but I agree with it," he answered.

When Milkowsky had quoted the line to Sara Dvayrah, she snapped, "A mouth like yours is an open-and-shut case, believe me!" and banged her feather duster in the air. The children sneezing behind him, Milkowsky could have pushed Sara into the wheezing refrigerator and smothered her mouth in the bruised tomatoes and blackening bananas of its vegetable bin. He went out and slammed the door in his wife's red face.

"Call me," Betty said.

The green sweater leaned in so close that Milkowsky could feel Betty Daugherty's breath, smell the peppermint lipstick. Her breath tickled his ear as she whispered, and her finger touched his thigh. Then she leaned back. In her eyes the young man saw curiosity. He was a sorry figure in his soiled blue shirt and shiny pants. The wool bunched over Betty's breasts as she reached across to the napkin holder, took one white napkin out, and scribbled a number on it. Pressing her lips to the wad of paper with a sideways smile, she rose in her seat.

"Are you taking me home?" the girl asked in the circle of smoke above the table.

One of the cabbies got up. "Sure." He gave Milkowsky a dirty look as he pushed past him, jingling his car keys. But she had gone by first, pushing the wad of paper into Milkowsky's palm. The hunched figure of the driver followed behind the girl. Her long legs flashed out from the short skirt and her feet arched even in the loafers she wore. She walked as if she were skating, and swung the suitcase that held her skates. Milkowsky wanted to get up, but he had to sit and be part of the fellowship of the table.

Landau was watching him. His face was sallow, yellow in the fluorescence of the cafeteria, brown in the sunlight. The blunt features buried in fat made Landau look Indian or African to outsiders who didn't recognize this type of Jew. The grease, the sadness of the all-night cafeteria pooled and ran down his pockmarked cheeks onto the floor, where the mops and slop buckets went around two or three times in the course of the night to wipe it up. The fat man would go to sleep on the plastic cushions surrounding the table of shouting, gesticulating politicians and truck drivers as if he had no home. He was awake now, though, and before Milkowsky could get up to run after Betty Daugherty with a question, Landau motioned him to keep his seat.

"How are you doing?" the accountant inquired.

Milkowsky shrugged his shoulders. The question had been asked in the voice Landau reserved for his persona in the synagogue. The fat man had dragged Milkowsky along once to make up the minyan, the ten bodies; and after offering some jokes in the last row, Landau had pushed himself out of his seat at the invitation of the old men and filled the basement prayer hall with a powerful trained baritone. It was in this deep voice that he now asked, "You want to make a dollar?"

"I just lost my job." Milkowsky spread his hands out to indicate helplessness.

"How much have you got in the bank?" Landau asked.

The taxi drivers and bookies were watching—Milkowsky felt pressure. "Four hundred dollars," he answered, faster than he should have, he thought, an instant after saying it.

"Give me three," Landau said sharply.

"What for?" Milkowsky's question asked itself among the guffaws around the table.

"I'm going to triple it for you." Landau was beaming, his fingers cracking back and forth as if shuffling a deck of cards.

"On the horses?" Milkowsky's voice cracked, knowing once he said yes, he would fall into an upside-down where Sara Dvayrah would pursue him, babies screaming at her girdle.

"I don't borrow for horses, Jerry," Landau half scolded. "Horses are metaphysical. This is business. Nothing can go wrong. It's money I have to have for a few weeks. But I can get it somewhere else."

From the narrow looks across the Formica surface, the suspension between the long jaws of the man who had tried to brush him away from the table, silence, Milkowsky knew that Landau had taken cash that night or the night before from everyone there. He understood, going back through the last hour's events, that Landau had brought the girl into his reach. Milkowsky was sick but he couldn't say anything but "Okay."

"Don't look so worried. It always hurts the first time." The table burst into coarse laughter at Landau's crack. The drivers began to tell stories of girls in the backs of their taxis, show-girls who wanted to take them to their hotel rooms or to go for a ride somewhere deep in the suburbs. How did these men, undersized or overweight, cynical, disheveled, their faces marked by pimples, scars, late-night wrinkles, inspire desire in the pink and fluffy dolls they described hailing them from stage doors? But there were so many details of Boston's streets, hotels, restaurants that Milkowsky believed them. Each tale left the men more deeply depressed, now that the girl was gone from the table. The words went around and the light lay bare each speaker's face.

Landau got up, sliding against the plastic stretched on the bolsters, grunting, and gestured to Milkowsky to walk out.

"Did you get her number?" the fat man asked.

"Yes," Milkowsky said, following his friend through the swinging doors of the cafeteria.

They walked toward the corner of Blue Hill and Morton, where Landau would turn left toward his rooms in an apartment, rooms rented from a widow. His wife had divorced him the same year he had been sent to the penitentiary. It was only a few minutes to the crossroads of the two large thoroughfares, a windy corner that displayed a drugstore at the northeast, one of the district's few bars to the southeast, across the way, a movie theater, and in the wake of these landmarks, a jeweler's, a travel agency, a hairdresser's shop, a driving school, a barbershop, all the enterprises that marked it as the hub of the Jewish streets, a self-contained community that sprawled over the political and geographical subdivisions of Boston, a town invisible on the highway maps, which could be easily drawn by running a pencil along the circumference of its farthest synagogues and delicatessens. This intersection, the busiest in the district, crowded with people and honking horns during the day, was now shut up in the three o'clock dark. Milkowsky noted that his companion was unusually quiet, which exaggerated the stillness. It was rare for Landau to go more than a few seconds in silence, unless he was asleep.

"Do you know her?" Milkowsky asked at last.

Landau didn't answer. He looked around at the silhouette of the houses and stores rising almost uniformly to a height of three stories like the façade of a Western town, south, up to Mattapan, and north, down to Franklin Field, just before the park. Milkowsky wondered why Landau had come back to the district where he was a comic figure. "The *frailichah gonif*," they called him in the synagogues. The white strings of Landau's short prayer shawl hung over the mouth of his pants pockets. They didn't tie him here, thought Milkowsky, a dozen cities had places to pray. Yet, as he stared at the fat man's girth, it seemed as if the strings, *tsittses,* were tiny, milky roots that held the bulk of the man, fed it from a spring under the cold gray slabs of cement, piercing the sidewalk.

When Landau turned around to talk, it was to discuss the details of receiving the cash. Milkowsky was to meet him in back of the small synagogue on Norfolk Street. It was a long walk for Milkowsky, but Landau was a regular there, doing business in the last rows and the men's room. The accountant was gloomy as he left the corner and walked alone up toward his two rooms on Morton Street.

Milkowsky's stomach was turning, the radishes on top of the herring, the tomatoes tossing in the brine. He knew he shouldn't give Landau the money. He considered hiding in bed through the next few days. The face of Betty Daugherty came toward him and he began to walk back in the direction of his house, up the Avenue, as if she were just ahead. A dozen scenes between them developed. He rose from her pillows dressed in sharp black woolen suits, fancy shoes, mono-grammed shirts—a hustler, a real-estate operator. The money he was going to give Landau became part of these snapshots: it tripled, quadrupled, folding itself over and over in a thick goatskin billfold.

Milkowsky went on past Wales Street, too excited to go home. The shadows of Dorchester's park began on the oppo-site side of the street. He crossed, walked through the entry to Franklin Park, beyond the wall of dressed brown stones, wan-dering in the grove of oaks to the brow of the hill overlooking the wide green meadows of the golf course. The streets of densely packed wooden three-deckers, their trash and red ash barrels, lay behind him in the Jewish ghetto. Through the wet April foliage, the rotten leaves, and the chives coming up, Jerry smelled the girl's body under its green sweater and short skirt. He took out the napkin, saw the red imprint of her lipstick in the moonlight, a kiss above the telephone number, and put it lightly to his own mouth, afraid to blot the writing.

It was morning when Milkowsky came up the front steps

on Wales Street. His daughters were already sitting at the table in front of bowls of cereal. Instead of rushing by, he sat down beside them and gave their ears a hard tug.

"What are you so happy about?" barked Sara Dvayrah, the big spoon from the bowl of porridge she had been stirring a menace in her fist. The bulk of his wife seemed like an asset to Milkowsky, in the light of the morning, an assurance, powerful, able to endure buffeting.

He looked up cheerfully and said, "A deal."

"What kind of a deal?" Sara dropped a dollop of oatmeal into one of the children's bowls to the sound of her last word.

"I'll tell you about it later," her husband said over his shoulder, pouring milk into the girls' portions.

"You'll tell me right now." Instead of stamping off or slipping away from the table, Milkowsky bent down and plucked up the baby. Tenderness toward her swollen red face rose like lust.

"How about some eggs?" he asked to the spoon threatening his ear.

"Eggs, eggs? What is this, a cafeteria?" Sara's voice rose.

Milkowsky laughed. "Why not?" He reached up and poked his wife in the stomach, then hugged the baby even harder.

Muttering, Sara Dvayrah went back to the stove.

Milkowsky got up from the table, smelling with pleasure the scent of eggs frying in the pan. He went into the bedroom to search for his single presentable suit, which hung in the closet. Laying it carefully over the back of a chair, he rifled the drawers in the bureau for socks, underwear, a clean white shirt, and, in the top chamber of the dresser, the bankbook. Milkowsky transferred this carefully to the inner pocket of the suit jacket, slipping the napkin from the old pair of pants in there as well, after checking that the number was still clear.

He came out to the breakfast table and patted his wife's rump, which swerved and almost upset the children's cereal bowls. Milkowsky carved then into soft yellow yolks.

The screams started a few minutes later and didn't even shake his fork. "The book, the book!" But Milkowsky was wiping his lips daintily and getting up, stroking the girls' heads, slipping two quarters apiece into their pockets.

Milkowsky telephoned Betty Daugherty later, in the afternoon. It was after he left Landau at the Norfolk Street shul. The accountant had been jolly when Milkowsky handed over the money in the leaky stalls of the men's room. "Look at you." Landau chuckled, putting his hands to the young man's neck, straightening the tie that hung there. "A real mensch. You see what lending out money turns you into—a banker."

Milkowsky smiled sourly. In fact, he had been happy since he had left his front door at eight in the morning, as Sara Dvayrah shouted at him, trying to catch hold of his lapels. Esther and Malkeh were comparing their shiny silver coins at the breakfast table, no longer confederates in the chase. And the baby, alert, was harrying her mother's leg in the doorway.

Inspired by a sense of the duties of his domestic establishment, Milkowsky had stopped in at a local insurance agency in the morning to ask about employment. After a cursory interview, the former lamp salesman sat in a cafeteria down the block from The New Yorker, making a list of employment possibilities on a napkin.

"Come into the toilet with me." Landau had leaned in close, his fleshy lips brushing Milkowsky's ear, so that the latter almost leaped in the pew. The soft, heavy fingers of the accountant's hand tugged at the breast pocket of his jacket. The gesture was too intimate and made Milkowsky shudder again, but he followed the direction of the pull at his chest, the fingers letting go only as he got up.

Landau bent over a cracked porcelain shell at the end of the stalls and, flushing the loud, antiquated plumbing, whispered into his companion's ear, "I may not be around for a while. Don't worry." He grinned broadly and licked his lips.

That was all. Abruptly he hurried away, leaving Milkowsky

listening to the toilet in front of him pumping, exploding, over and over. When he walked out a few moments later to ask Landau what he meant, the synagogue was empty except for its caretaker, who warded off inquiries with a head that shook slightly to whatever question was asked of it, locked in an inner dialogue with angel or palsy.

To the ringing telephone, dialed at four o'clock from the corner of Morton and Norfolk, there was no answer.

The shadows began to swallow up the afternoon light in the phone booth as Milkowsky tried again and again, feeling more foolish and awkward each time the ring echoed. Ten, eleven, twelve alarms—the painful tugging in his chest was succeeded by the stubborn sounding of the bell, until Milkowsky finally banged the receiver back into its cradle. He dialed again. He was ready to quit when he caught the first of the busy signals.

It was twilight. A sky spotted like a bloody slab of salmon shone in the west window of the phone booth. Milkowsky, relieved from the constant dialing, ringing, buzzing, was shaking. The wind had turned cold and without the sun it was now chilly in the iron-and-glass rectangle. The rhythm of dragging the circle around the dial box and the stinging, clammy echo of the receiver had been pressing in and out of Milkowsky's ear for the past two hours. Suddenly Betty Daugherty's voice broke in. "Hello," she said.

"Hello?" Milkowsky responded.

He asked it as if no one were on the other end. In the long silence, after hearing again the soft languorous pronunciation come up from below her larynx, the breath sighing through the *h* and the foggy vibration of the *o,* the young man was afraid Betty would hang up, and he fumbled forward. "It's Jerry." The sound that greeted this was barely audible; it was inhaled, drawn through the teeth close to the receiver in South Boston or Irish Dorchester adjoining, it whistled.

Milkowsky held on to the telephone, afraid that she had

forgotten who he was or that she had been drunk and was not capable at that moment of remembering.

"How are you?"

He heard a rap against the side of the telephone booth. But it was Betty's voice asking.

"Terrible," he answered. He waited for the inevitable "Why?" from the girl, but it didn't come. The rap struck a second time, louder. "I've been dreaming about you," he said, beginning to get desperate.

"Is that so terrible?" The force of her voice, suddenly clear, resonating in the bell of the telephone, struck him through the forehead. He hung dumb against the wall, until he realized how long his silence had filled the receiver.

"N . . . no, it isn't." Milkowsky faltered.

"What do you want?" she asked.

"Y . . . you said to call," he stammered, wondering if the girl had just been teasing him.

"Yes," she answered, very matter-of-factly.

"I want to see you," he said.

"Well." He couldn't tell from Betty's answer whether she was encouraging him or not.

A face appeared in the glass of the telephone booth, cherry lipstick thick as jam smeared down onto the chin. The cheeks were spotted with clumps of powder, orange dots on pale white. Black eyelashes batted under plucked-out brows penciled crudely with waving black lines.

"When?" Milkowsky asked. His heart turned upside down.

"When do you want to see me?" she asked, half impatient.

"Tonight?" He felt his voice get shrill.

"Jerry!" The voice, high-pitched, drowned out the response on the other end of his line.

"Tonight?" he asked again.

"I told you already," Betty answered. "I can't."

"Tomorrow?"

"It's no good the rest of the week. I've got something happening," the girl said.

"What?" Milkowsky felt foolish asking, but he couldn't help himself.

"Why do you want to know?" Betty was not so much brusque as amused.

"I want to know *you*," he answered, hoping to get the conversation on a more personal level.

"Jerry . . ." Betty's voice was husky, and it made him shiver in the space of the booth.

"Next week?" He couldn't help the tone of begging that crept in.

"Sure," Betty replied. And then she whispered, her voice a little hoarse, "I want to know *you*."

"Jerry!" It was a scream of agony, the lips were wiping in scarlet strokes back and forth on the glass. A fist began to hammer.

"I . . ." Milkowsky tried to talk, but he felt as if the Irish girl had unbuttoned her dress to him, and he was floating in dizzy heat, not believing what he heard, even as he strained to keep the door shut.

"Talk to me . . ." he whispered into the receiver. What he heard back was husky, cajoling, funny, but it was drowned out by the shriek—"Jerry!"

The glass fell in, and arms wound with brass bracelets, hairy, bleeding where bits of the glass were sticking in them, shook in his face, fingers grabbing for the earphone.

"Jerry?" Betty said.

"Jerry!" the shriek cut in.

"What is it?" Betty asked, aware of the interruption.

"It's my mother." Milkowsky cried into the phone, unable to hear himself as he wrestled the woman's fingers away from the receiver and the cord she was trying to rip out.

"Your *what*?" But Betty's voice was so faint in the clamor of the booth he couldn't distinguish what she was saying or hope to maintain the conversation.

"Can I call you back?" he shouted. "Later?"

He thought he heard "Yes," and laughter.

The receiver was swaying in the air.

"Take me home! Take me home! Jerry!" The stocky woman had given up clutching at the phone and snatched at his lapels. She was coming through the folding door. Milkowsky thought he heard a voice call from the receiver, but it was dead when he caught it, a moment before he was gathered into breasts, lipstick, blood in his teeth. "The babies," his mother wailed between kisses. "I want to see my babies!"

Sara Dvayrah had forbidden her to enter the house since the last visit almost two years before when the older woman had pulled off all her clothes and frightened the little girls. Sara, pregnant with her third, was beside herself and had almost lost the six-month fetus. There were false labor pains, bleeding, other mysterious symptoms that filled the house with panic and brought Jerry's father to the doctors' offices at the mental-health institution in Mattapan to beg for the strict confinement of his wife over the next months. The offices, in a shining modern building with light streaming through wide plate glass on bright plastic chairs, overlooked a series of crumbling brick dormitories whose walls were spotted with human droppings.

It was impossible to keep all the patients locked up inside on a twenty-four-hour basis without a rise in mortality rates. Mrs. Milkowsky was one of the healthier, outgoing, rapturous spirits in Mattapan. The staff liked her enthusiasm, the flashes of philosophical insight into her condition. She had the freedom of the grounds. The iron fence fell to the sidewalk some three hundred yards from the gate and thereafter sank its teeth, spears, into the soil of the rolling fields, the roots of wild onion grass and Ponca arrowheads. It offered no bar to ingress or egress. Mrs. Milkowsky was welcome to adventure to Wyoming. Only parental duties tied her to adjoining streets. She was solicitous for her child, her grandchildren. "Perhaps," the doctors suggested, smiling, smoothing the wrinkles out of their white-jacketed arms, tugging at the cuffs, "his daughter-in-law ought to try to think about her mother-in-law's actions in a kinder light, a demonstration of affection, concern, an attempt to get into the act."

"Maybe Sara would like some counseling?" one of the aides suggested.

Sara's father-in-law rose nervously, eyeing the exit. He thanked the doctors profusely, but it was time, he explained, glancing at his wristwatch, for the afternoon services. He couldn't be missed.

Instead, the elder Milkowsky had taken to sitting on the front porch of the house where his son occupied the upper floor, in a broken wooden chair, hoping to ward off his wife, who was afraid of the quiet little man who had slouched after her in sad shoes and threadbare socks from one step to another. Her husband's patient glance of disappointment, his look to the floor that found no voice between his pursed, thin lips, but could be heard against the linoleum sounding board, a narrowed breath plucking nostril hairs, its vibration through her cupboard—this set her to screaming, crying. Wherever her husband sat a shadow squatted, and Mrs. Milkowsky would hurry away to the other side of the street.

"Jerry! Jerry!" The young man felt her, warm, trembling, holding him tight, patting his cheek. He breathed the sour breath through the sticky smear of her lipstick, the perfume sprinkled in his mother's cheeks. "Let me! Let me!"

He tried to hug her. "Momma. Momma."

"Let me," Mrs. Milkowsky insisted.

"You can't," her son answered.

"You *momzer*. Bastard." She tore his suit lapel with the strength of a wrestler. "You're killing me." She struck him in the face with her fist as he tried to pry her fingers from his jacket, and the blow knocked him off balance in the booth. He fell sideways and felt the hard kicking of her high heels. "Killer," she was screaming. "Killer."

A siren wailed under her high-pitched staccato. "You're killing me. Stop it! Stop it!"

Milkowsky was shielding his face from the kick when a

blue-uniformed arm reached in and yanked him hard by the elbow. "Get up!"

"You want to *kill* me?" the stocky woman screamed outside the booth.

"Look . . ." Milkowsky knocked his head against the top of the door frame as he was pulled out onto Morton Street. He had reached for his mother's face as if to stop her mouth, but the baton of the short, broad-backed policeman came down on his wrist. The young man raised his hand again in what was meant as a gesture of explanation, but the baton slammed.

"He's a killer!" Mrs. Milkowsky cried out, trying to swing at her son, too, with an oversized pocketbook she had retrieved from the sidewalk.

"What did he try to do?" A second cop, taller and heavier than the first, called from behind the woman, his baton out.

"Look at me," she said, "look."

"You're a mess," the tall cop sympathized. "Did he mess you up?"

"He stole," she whispered loudly.

"You're a little pig," the voice whispered in Milkowsky's ear. "Pickin' on an old lady?" The wooden stick cracked, punctuating the question.

She ripped open the purse and showed its empty, torn silk lining. "Nothing. He stole from me."

"Where is it?" the cop asked, and his arm seized, then shook Milkowsky.

Milkowsky's throat was full of phlegm and bitter water, and he felt pain over the bridge of his nose where the rod had hit him at the end of the question. The tall cop came forward and began to frisk the young man, turning the pockets of his pants and jacket inside out.

"In his house!" the woman on the curb volunteered.

"His house?" The police looked at the woman, her bright, smeared lipstick, oversized dress, thickly powdered cheeks.

"My babies," she explained. "He stole my babies."

"She's my mother." Milkowsky spoke into the silence on Morton and Norfolk.

A shadow crossed Mrs. Milkowsky's face. She drew herself up stiffly and said, "Take me home."

"You can't go home, Momma," Milkowsky said, exasperated, plaintive.

"Why can't she?" asked the tall cop.

"She's not well," Milkowsky tried to explain.

"What's the matter?" The policeman was suspicious.

Milkowsky shook his head. "I want to go home," his mother repeated.

"I can't," Milkowsky replied. "You know that."

"We'll take you home, lady. Where do you live?" the shorter of the two policemen reassured her.

"You can't," her son cut in.

"Wales Street," the mother replied in a voice loud enough to be heard over her son's.

"She doesn't." Milkowsky was angry now.

"Where does she live, then?" the tall cop asked.

"He doesn't want . . ." Mrs. Milkowsky spoke rapidly.

"Mattapan," Milkowsky shouted. "Do you understand? The mental . . . Mattapan!"

The April wind swept around the two policemen, the young husband, his mother, a telephone booth, kicking bits of paper up and into the gutter.

"Do you want to call?" All the anger had run off into Milkowsky's throat. "Cunningham 6-4 . . ."

"You believe him?" The firmness in his mother's voice was betrayed by an echo of appeal.

The policeman looked again at her makeup, false eyelashes, the contrast of her white cheeks spotted with orange dots under which ran a blue scar, a real and sinister slash. The hem of her dress slumped lower, farther out of fashion, stains and patches stood out in the hand-me-down. She shivered. "You want my coat?" asked the short policeman.

"Thank you," she answered primly.

"Why don't the two of you get in and we'll clear this up in a jiffy," said the tall cop.

"Couldn't we stop?" she asked as the car with flashing lights crossed over the Avenue. "Just to see."

The policemen looked back to Milkowsky beside her in the rear of the car. He bit his lip and, sinking his head, mumbled, "It isn't me."

"Mrs. Milkowsky. *Faites-moi le plaisir?*" At the door of the reception facility, the young doctor came down a few steps and took the older woman's hand. She was drying her tears with the handkerchief one of the men in the squad car had given her and barely acknowledged the doctor's greeting.

"You'll see 'em. I'm gonna say a novena for yuh." The tall policeman patted her free hand and, bending across her, shot at the doctor, "Why can't she go home?"

The doctor flicked his wrist back above the cuff of a white dressing gown and opened his palm. "The family." A slight smile crossed the policeman's features as he looked hard at Milkowsky, the bruises on his face and the torn lapel.

"You don't"—Milkowsky tried to articulate the next word—"understand."

"It's your mother," said the tall cop, cutting off the end of the son's remark.

The blue figure turned on his heel. Milkowsky followed him out to the squad car to explain, but the door was slammed in his face and the automobile sped away.

The sky was black as Milkowsky made his way on the sidewalk opposite the iron pickets. This part of the fence for the Mattapan State Institute for Mental Health still stood erect. The pavement rolled and buckled as it climbed a hillside buried under trees and houses. The city had neglected to repair the sidewalk here for many years and plates of cement had been shifted this way and that under the winter frost heaves. It was colder than the night before and Milkowsky tried to warm up by breaking into a run. There was a telephone at the corner of Harvard and Blue Hill, ahead, in a drugstore.

Milkowsky had asked Sara Dvayrah to let him bring the girls to visit their grandmother at Mattapan. She refused. The children didn't want to go—the smell of the wards, urine, excrement, and the green institutional paint flaking on the walls unsettled them. It was a zoo full of animals looming dangerously close to their faces, and the surprises were all frightening. Mrs. Milkowsky's illness had happened so gradually in her son's own childhood that he didn't understand how sick she was until the ambulance came one night. The screaming, the bursts of singing, dancing, dirty words, long silent sulks in the kitchen, his father's labored breathing had gone on since he could remember. Shut up in the walls of the apartment, he felt it as a relief when one of the partners had been taken away, but his father had faded from the rooms, too, in the wake of his mother's confinement. The tailor had retired early and become religious, thinner, more taciturn, as his wife got fat, talked faster and faster. Milkowsky went rarely to Mattapan. Every time he met his mother accidentally in the street, there was a scene. Yet he felt bad. His mother had held his hand tight when he was a little boy, dropped everything when he ran in with a scratch or a bleeding nose after a fall or a fight with the bullies down the street. It was she who would run out with a frying pan and threaten to murder his tormentors. His father's pants had been threshed for nickels to give to the boy, and she tried to cook, though she lost patience in the middle, distractedly left things to burn, repeatedly rushed back to a smoking oven.

Only once had the boy heard his father complain. The result was something Milkowsky had not understood: crying, the telephone, police arriving at the house, his mother gone for the night, and his father, walking, walking, up and down the long corridor of the apartment, through the evening into the morning, over a carpet in which flowers—deep blue, purple, orange, flecked with white diamonds and stars zigzagging through a wine-red field—that had been pointed out to him in childhood now faded into a muddy remnant worn bare to the cross fibers of its backing on the passageway floor.

The green barracks at the corner of Harvard and Blue Hill, which housed an ice-cream fountain, a pinball arcade, and a pharmacy under the same roof, were lit up in front of Milkowsky like a crystal palace. He shook off his lethargy and bolted through the Avenue traffic. The store was half deserted and he went right to the telephone.

His fingers fumbled back and forth in the lining of his suit jacket for the napkin. It wasn't in the side pockets of his pants either. Milkowsky began to feel a tremor come up his back as he reached out to the side for the Boston telephone book. There were columns of Daughertys, but no Betty. There was a B. Daugherty, and though the digits didn't seem familiar he dialed them. A coarse voice, an old man's, answered: "Hello?"

"Is Betty Daugherty there?" the young man asked.

"Sure. Who is it?" The harsh lilt of second-generation Irish, of a longshoreman or teamster, sounded through the receiver in the Dorchester drugstore.

"She's about eighteen, twenty, right?" Milkowsky added, hoping it was the right house.

"What business is it of yours?" inquired the man at the other end, suddenly wary.

"I met her last . . ." Milkowsky tried to explain.

"The hell you did. What's your name?" the voice asked, gruff. Milkowsky let the receiver slam back into place. The pharmacist looked at him suspiciously between the pillars of aspirins, suppositories, and liver pills framing the cash register. Milkowsky realized he had made a fool of himself. He had to go back to Morton and Norfolk, where the police had shaken him down . . . see if the paper had blown into the gutter or was pasted into a pile of leaves.

It was two in the morning when Milkowsky came home. He had gone by The New Yorker, but none of the cabbies knew where Betty Daugherty was or where she lived. The man who had dropped her off was nowhere in sight. The drivers Milkowsky recognized from the night before wanted to know only where Meyer was, and an ugly tide of murmurs flowed around the circle as the young man stood on one foot, then the other, hoping someone would volunteer some information about Betty.

"You know him pretty well, huh?" a little man, cap cocked back and to the side, burst out as Milkowsky hung on at the entrance to the round table.

"Who?" Milkowsky asked, not really paying attention.

"What are you, a wise guy?" A big man, a thug at the local pool hall, cut in, his voice threatening.

"Landau?" asked Milkowsky, suddenly aware that the situation was becoming dangerous.

"You're his buddy," said the pool shark.

"I don't know him any better than you," Milkowsky protested, starting to back away.

"You knew he was leaving," the shark, looming over him, said, blocking his way. Milkowsky's face went white as he felt the anger of the table moving up toward him. He knew these men were numbers runners, bookies. One of his schoolmates had been badly beaten after crossing them, and left Boston without teeth. "He took my money this afternoon," Milkowsky exclaimed, hoping to establish his credit. The cabby who had spoken to him in the first place looked at the torn lapel of Jerry's suit jacket and grimaced.

"Why don't you get lost!" the short driver said, pushing his cap back on his head.

Milkowsky understood that they believed him—he was just a schmo. He hurried away.

"Where were you?" Sara Dvayrah was waiting up in the kitchen as he came through the door.

"My mother . . ." said Milkowsky.

"Your mother . . . at two in the morning!" she shouted.

Standing in front of his heavy wife—dumpy, slatternly under her flannel nightshirt—Milkowsky wanted to hit. Take a table leg, a broom handle, whip that flesh falling into rings of depression, wake her up. To club—not Sara, but what was happening, suffocating, choking him. She took a step back in front of his raised arm.

"You killer," he said, the words barely audible. "You killer." Before Sara could scream, waking the girls, Milkowsky backed away, blundered into the bedroom, fell down on the bed, sleep overcoming him as he touched the raised embroidery of the spread.

"The money," Sara screamed in his face. It was eight o'clock in the morning. "What did you do with the money?" Jerry realized he had never gotten under the sheets and was still in his clothes. "The money!"

He pulled himself out of bed and headed for the door. His father was in the living room, silent, a grim look on his face. He got up mournful. "Jerry."

"I'm going," he screamed at the older man.

"No, no," his father began, a look of pain distorting the set lines of despair.

"I'm going to get a job. A job!" Milkowsky slammed the door on them.

Why didn't he run? Landau had run. Milkowsky had the bankbook in his pocket. There was a hundred dollars or more left. A bus would get him to New York. Or he could just show up in Mattapan and lie down beside his mother. He began to breathe heavily. The bastards, *momzers*. They had stolen the number, his number. He began to cry, deep throbbing cries that came up from his stomach. He leaned on the banister of a neighboring three-decker's front step and held on while the spasms shook him. Nothing, he had nothing.

"Jerry."

He turned around and looked into his father's drawn, pale face. "I'm sorry," the little man whispered, then swung around and hobbled away as quickly as he could.

In the next weeks, Milkowsky worked as a dishwasher, a window scrubber, a stock boy and delivery boy for the local Stop & Shop, climbing to the top floors of the houses up and down the nearby streets.

He did not exchange a word with Sara. Esther and Malkeh, afraid of them both, played quiet games in the corners of the apartment when called inside. A single sentence threatened to ignite the gas leaking from the burners. Milkowsky came home exhausted, threw most of the money he had earned into a bowl on the living-room table, took off his clothes, fell asleep. It was Sara who was sleeping on the living-room couch now. Milkowsky asked to work extra shifts, weekends, went to the grocery on Sundays to help do inventory, rearrange the stock, wash the floors.

He was dreaming again, he realized as he found himself at the end of the fourth week of work, walking down Harvard Street past the intersection of Wales, down the Avenue. He was headed for the windows of The New Yorker, even though it was after dark and he had worked two shifts that day in the aisles, stacking cans. He tried to turn himself around, but it was too late, and he passed the wall of Franklin Field, the gloomy deserted field house, the windows of dry cleaners, fruit stores, bakeries, the zipper factory, a Hebrew bookstore, before he knew what had happened. He turned his nose against the thick glass of The New Yorker's broad windows on Blue Hill and stared through the blinds at the customers.

The crew of bookies and petty criminals was at its customary round table. Milkowsky recognized squeezed in among them the taxi driver who had taken Betty home; he was stirring a cup of coffee with his middle finger. Milkowsky pushed through the chipped glass doors of the cafeteria.

"Hi!" The table looked up at his greeting, incredulous, as if a girl in high heels had wandered into the fetid stalls of the men's room downstairs.

"Remember me?" Milkowsky asked the driver, but no one at the table looked up again. He had no business at this table. It didn't exist for him.

Milkowsky reached out and touched the hairy backside of the man's hand. "That girl . . . Betty?"

Two narrow eyes, flecked with spots of gray and blood, looked up at Milkowsky as the finger came out of the mud of coffee grinds and dissolved sugar. "What about her?" the driver barked.

"Do you know her number?" Milkowsky asked.

"What for?" In the cabby's question there was a lewd suggestion that scratched the formica.

"I gotta give her something," the young man whispered.

"Give it to me!" The hairy arm came up at him.

"I promised it in person," Milkowsky said quickly.

"What's it worth?" A muddy finger dangled under Milkowsky's nose.

"Twenty." He felt a lump in his throat as he bartered.

"Twenty?" The cabby's voice was incredulous.

"Fifty?" Milkowsky pulled out his wallet. "It's all I got."

"Forget her," said the taxi man, slamming his fist down.

The table laughed, sideways, so as not to acknowledge the young man bending over it, but to applaud the other man's joke. "Please." Milkowsky cut in.

"She's a real bummer. Forget her," the man repeated between the laughter wheezing in the seats.

"I'll . . ." Milkowsky was about to offer money he didn't have in his pocket.

"I forgot . . . I tried *hard*." The driver lowered his finger back into the cup and Milkowsky swung around, afraid of the other looks he was getting.

The skating rink across the Avenue was open. Milkowsky crossed over and walked through the front doors. There were two dozen girls skating in the cavernous space and a few boys. None of them looked like Betty Daugherty, although his heart began to beat so hard that he noticed it, as the fifteen- and sixteen-year-olds whirled by the edge of the stand in skirts that left their thighs bare. In the flash of white, muscular intimacy he imagined Betty, touching her, the two of them in her sheets. In the warmth of this, Milkowsky felt he was being stared at, too, and, looking to the right, saw that he had attracted the hostile look of a young man resting on his skates at the edge of the rink and an older man, a father perhaps, perched in the upper rows. The cashier behind him began to cough, and Milkowsky turned around and walked out, before someone asked him what he wanted there.

Back on the Avenue, he started for Wales Street, wondering if he could learn to skate. He was passing the wall of Franklin Field, a long, dark stretch, when someone grabbed him from behind and forced him to the right, off the sidewalk of Blue Hill, onto a path toward the shadows of the boarded-up field house. "Just keep quiet," a voice growled, "and you won't get hurt."

"Okay, okay," he agreed, frightened.

He was pushed down a flight of steps and shoved against a locked doorway. "Where's Meyer?" the man demanded.

"I don't know," Milkowsky squeaked.

"What did he tell you?" The voice behind him was one of those from the table at The New Yorker, but Milkowsky couldn't connect it to a face.

"Nothing," he pleaded.

"What did he *tell* you?" the man behind him growled. Milkowsky's arm, which had been pinned behind his back, was twisted so that he began to shout. *"What?"* growled the hood.

"He was going away," the young man gasped.

"Where?"

"He took my money, *too*."

Later Milkowsky remembered a few other questions before the blow that blacked everything out. The police found him and he woke up in the squad car. His face was covered with blood from the cut in his scalp. "It's just superficial," the cops told him. His wallet had been emptied. "You wanna go to the hospital?" they asked at the station. They had called his wife and told her not to worry. Dazed, Milkowsky asked them just to take him home. One of the policemen he recognized from The New Yorker, a guy who often sat at the round table; he seemed to be eyeing Jerry with a smirk.

The few dollars Milkowsky had set aside over the last few weeks and his whole salary were in the wallet. It would be a month before he had enough for a bus ticket to New York City and a few days' stake in a hotel room with meals. What was the point? The point! He climbed the stairs at Wales Street wanting to kill someone, the cops, the taxi driver, himself. He brushed by Sara, who stood without greeting him at the door, and went into the bedroom and fell onto the bed, lapsing into sleep as if someone had slugged him again.

In the middle of the dark, Milkowsky heard a piercing wail and started awake. It was the baby crying. Usually Sara Dvayrah's footsteps followed the call of one of the children, and he had learned to sleep through it or doze back into dreams. The wailing continued, but the house did not respond. After a few minutes, he rose and walked toward the corridor where the crib was wedged for lack of another bedroom. The baby's face was contorted and red with tears. He picked her up and she stopped crying, grabbing at the linen lapel of his grocery smock, hugging him. Drawing the little girl close, Milkowsky made his way back to the bed, where he slept alone, and fell asleep with the child snoring quietly in the crook of his arm.

"Get up!" In the morning, Sara, standing over Milkowsky, roughly pushed his elbow in the bed. She gathered up the baby, who complained drowsily, still asleep, and set the tiny head against her breasts. "There's a call for you."

He hurried into the living room. It was the insurance agent on the line. Did Milkowsky want to come down and talk about a job? "Sure, sure." He would be there in an hour, Milkowsky answered, trying to sound enthusiastic, his head still thick and banging.

His suit was in the closet. When he took it out, he noticed that the lapel was still ripped to the side, where it hung like a limp flipper. Sara Dvayrah was sitting in the narrow galley of the kitchen. He walked in with the jacket. "Can you sew it?"

She took it without speaking, went back into the bedroom for the sewing box, and sat silently working her needle in the living room at the apartment's largest table. Milkowsky thought he saw tears in her eyes. Sara's hands were buried in the work. When she got up he went over to take it, but she brushed by him and went into the kitchen, and then returned with an iron. She pressed the jacket into a neat, fresh appearance without a wrinkle.

What had happened?

Milkowsky remembered a tart-tongued girl two years younger than he, around whom the neighborhood boys had not begun to swarm since her breasts were still modest under her pink Orlon sweaters. But Sara had smooth creamy skin with pink dots in her cheeks, and a pert, girlish figure.

Jerry had had a crush on Sara when he was still staggering around the yard of the Boston Latin Public School, a kid spouting Nietzsche, Sartre, Spinoza. One late May afternoon toward dusk, when the trees were full of green wings floating to the white concrete pavements, he sat down beside her on the steps. On the tip of his tongue were quotations from the texts passed around among his circle of friends at the bottom of the class—rebels, *Ausländer*. After one or two false starts, the words were caught in the warm spring air and sailed off to the tops of the trees, where they dangled from the branches sticky with new leaves. Sara watched him as he spoke and waved his arms. He could feel, in the way the thirteen-year-old leaned forward, with her thumb and forefinger cradling her chin, that she liked him.

"Do you always talk to girls like this?" Sara asked.

"How?" he responded, taken aback.

"From books." She looked into his black eyes, which started to twitch.

"How should I talk?" Jerry was at a loss for a smart remark.

"I don't know."

"Kiss me," Jerry said, bluffly, his cheeks coloring red.

"Not here," Sara answered, her face blank.

Milkowsky was surprised. He had half risen, expecting she would turn away from his bravado. This was as good as a promise.

"Where?" he asked, lowering his voice.

"Let's go for a walk," Sara said. She looked off down the street as if they had been sitting long enough.

"Okay." Jerry straightened up and took a step away.

"Not now." She laughed for the first time. "Are you in such a rush?"

"When?" He was unable to conceal his eagerness.

"Am I too young for you?" The question came after a long pause. She seemed to step back.

"No." Jerry blushed more deeply.

"Come and see me tomorrow," Sara said quickly.

"Why?" Jerry wasn't sure whether he had a date with her.

"Maybe—" Her look was blank.

"Maybe what?" He rocked back and forth on his heels, feeling himself getting itchy, wanting to touch her.

"I may be older," she said with a half smile.

"Do you love me?" Jerry asked without meaning to.

"Love you?" Sara looked quizzical. "Are you okay?"

"I'm just teasing," he answered, snorting in his nose.

"I hope so."

It made Jerry flush to be put down by someone who despite the curves of her calves and thighs was still almost an infant in the eyes of his peers. He got up to move on, not sure he would be back the next afternoon, when a sharp stone stung his cheek. He wheeled around to see her laughing at him, but before he turned angrily away, he heard her call, "I *like* you."

Sara did let him kiss her, not the next day, but a week later, as she teased him but made him feel that she wanted to see him. Her mother was a widow who worked behind the counter in a local drugstore and Sara was alone on the front steps through that spring and summer. As the white and green fuzz of her woolen pullovers stretched before her developing bosom, the boys began to stick to the stoop of the wooden three-decker, but she would put out her hand and pull Jerry next to her, to let him know she liked him best. He got some kidding from the other guys in his gang for going out with a girl two years younger, especially when the next year one of the older boys got hold of a car and began to drive the group out to wealthy suburbs for dates.

At fifteen, Sara was one of the prettiest girls in Dorchester, although she was already showing weight in her arms and around her waist, the effects of free sweets from the glass cases of the pharmacy and the ice-cream cones where she was working beside her mother.

Jerry wasn't accepted to an Ivy League school. Most of his grades were mediocre and his father didn't have the money for tuition. As a junior and senior in high school, Jerry spent most of his time dreaming in class, thinking of hugging his girl-friend, who was affectionate but careful not to let him get beyond putting thumbs under her brassiere. Her prominent front made the other local boys poke elbows in Jerry's side during street-corner meetings, and he didn't enlighten them about the limits. At college Jerry might have broken off. Sara was attractive, but now there were other girls. Her mother died suddenly, and a few weeks later Sara let him keep moving under her clothes with his hands until, as she squirmed and hugged him, it happened.

Jerry was married and a father before he understood what was behind him. College became almost impossible. He took courses at night or tried to arrange job hours around lectures he was attending during the day. Sara worked until the labor pains began. She went back to the pharmacy as soon as a babysitter could be found. Mrs. Milkowsky volunteered to look after the infant, but her husband discouraged it. The grandmother's excited giggling in front of the baby upset both of the new parents. When the second daughter was born, in Jerry's senior year, Sara stayed home for good. There was no money for Jerry to go on to a professional school, and his grades were barely adequate for graduation.

Milkowsky got the job. He held it. It seemed he had a knack for selling insurance. "What are you afraid of? What do you think might happen? What could go wrong? What do you want to see?" Questions that were strange in a lamp store fit right in with policies for disaster.

He bought another suit, better. His hours kept him out of The New Yorker, and for a while, angry and afraid, he avoided the place. The roller rink, too, seemed out of bounds. Sara was making an effort at home. She started to diet, lose weight. She talked about going back to school when the baby was old enough to go off for a full day of nursery school. She asked her husband what he wanted to eat.

Meanwhile, Milkowsky began to take the baby off for walks on Sunday afternoons. He strolled through Franklin Park, smelling the trees, grass, letting the baby romp; then, scooping her onto his shoulders, he crossed out of the park, over the highway to the south, through the back yard of the Jewish Community Center to Lorne Street, Harvard Street, and on to the gates of the state mental hospital. His mother cried and jumped around a lot the first time, but the nurses were considerate and the baby seemed to like the attention.

"I saw my mother yesterday," Milkowsky told his wife, after a month and a half of visits.

Sara nodded. "The baby talks about it."

He looked up, surprised. "She's been saying *bobbeh*," his wife added with an indulgent lift of the eyebrow.

The fussing, the cuddling, the candy for the baby had resulted in a reward. Her benefactress got the baby's first word, *bobbeh*, grandmother. Milkowsky, sitting by himself in the hospital lobby, reading the free magazines, had not heard it. Seeing the little bags of jelly beans, the other treats she now brought back on Sunday, the baby's two sisters became interested in their grandmother and began to visit with their father on odd weekends. There was no discussion. Sara had stopped shouting. Milkowsky realized that he was being deferred to.

"I hear you and the girls saw your mother," his father said, meeting him one day on the way to work.

Milkowsky nodded, looking down. His father patted his hand. In spite of himself, Milkowsky was moved and felt his eyes mist. "She seems okay."

His father lowered his eyes and stared at the sidewalk. After a moment's awkward silence, he looked at his son. "You want a cup of coffee?"

"No, the office is opening in a few minutes. Thanks, though. Maybe later."

"Good, good. No, it's good. You have to be there bright and early." The tailor, his face creased with a hundred wrinkles, looked up with the shyest of smiles. "Have a good day," he said, and hurried away.

As Milkowsky sat at his desk that morning, the phone rang. "I want some insurance."

"Fine." Milkowsky leaned back in his chair, a pad in his lap, a pencil in his hand.

"A lot."

"Great," the salesman chimed in enthusiastically.

"How much can I buy?" The caller was anxious.

"How much do you want?" Milkowsky cheerfully implied that there were no limits.

"Life insurance." The voice checked cautiously.

"Okay," Milkowsky confirmed. He was ready to write.

"More than I can afford." The pencil flipped in Milkowsky's fingers. "Someone wants to kill me." There was no sound. Then: "Will it pay me?"

"Meyer?" Milkowsky recognized the deep, booming laugh.

"How much?" the CPA shouted through the merry waves shaking him on the other end.

"Where are you?" Milkowsky asked.

"Across the street. I saw you sitting in the window a second ago," Landau confided.

"Where?" Milkowsky looked out between his blinds.

"I got your money, don't worry, what do you . . ."

"They . . ." Milkowsky broke in.

"I paid them already." Landau's assurance cut off his friend's anxious whisper. "Come on out, I tripled it for you. Have a cup of coffee. Meet me at The New Yorker." Milkowsky picked up his briefcase and waved to his employer. Landau was standing at the doorway of the cafeteria. The place was half deserted. It was the middle of the morning—too late for bagels, eggs, too early for corned-beef sandwiches and pickles. The accountant looked heavier but was bundled into a pin-striped suit that made him appear almost smart. He gave Milkowsky a pinch on the cheek. "I made you. I made you. Look at you, a real mensch! I'm not kidding. I need some insurance, life insurance."

Meyer pushed him into a side booth and slid a shiny leather case out of his breast pocket. "Look!" He opened it and peeled nine hundred-dollar bills off a green packet, reaching into Milkowsky's jacket and stuffing them into his shirt.

"You thought I ran away on you. Listen, I did. And I have to keep moving." The accountant looked around with flashing eyes, watching the entrance, the door to the kitchen, the stairs to the men's room. "I didn't pay *everybody*."

They got up. Landau reached back for the last bit of the bagel left on his plate. "You can't get these to taste right in California. I'm going to call you." They exited the cafeteria. Landau shook Milkowsky's hand and began to walk quickly down the side street, where someone was waiting for him behind the wheel of a black Cadillac.

"Listen," Milkowsky said, "that girl, Betty . . ."

"Betty!" cried Landau. He motioned Milkowsky to stay where he was, not to follow him to the car, and swung open the door and squeezed himself into the back seat. "Our highest insights must, should . . . sound like . . . crimes," he shouted from the window as the car sped away. "I'll call."

Walking back past the door of The New Yorker, Milkowsky saw a taxi screech to a halt in front of the door and double-park. The driver, the same one who had taken Betty home that night, bolted out into the restaurant. Milkowsky crossed the Avenue quickly and headed back to his office. The precise cut of his blue wool blazer and gray flannel pants made him invisible to the men of the night tables when the cabbies crossed his path on the late-afternoon sidewalk. The insurance agent's costume belonged to a world they barely acknowledged.

Soon Jerry Milkowsky would disappear entirely. The daytime bustle of the Jewish streets was on the move to other places. The agency was about to open a branch in Newton, where many of its better customers were moving. The owner had approached Milkowsky about taking charge of that office and offered a small share of the business if everything worked out. The nine hundred dollars he had gotten from Landau tipped a decision seesawing for the last month. The apartment was too small. The youngest girl needed a bedroom. The two older ones were still sleeping in the dining-room alcove. Milkowsky, who was bringing work home, wanted a study where he could go over figures without the children racing around his feet. With a loan and his savings over the year and a half at the insurance agency, in another six months he could afford a mortgage for a modest house on one of the older, less affluent Newton streets; he could walk to work at the agency. It would be difficult to get back to Mattapan and Dorchester to see his mother and father, but when he broached the idea to Sara Dvayrah, she offered to take Mrs. Milkowsky for a weekend once a month. There would be a cot for Mr. Milkowsky whenever he wanted to visit.

When they moved a year later, Milkowsky had been commuting eight months by bus to Newton. Their new house had a big back yard for the children to play in, separate rooms for each of the girls, a study, a dining room. Milkowsky had been selling a lot of insurance and the commissions were substantial. He took the day off before the movers came, to help Sara Dvayrah bundle papers, books, and clothes into boxes and sacks. In the middle of the afternoon he heard Sara cry from the other room, "Oh, God, I forgot."

"What is it?" Milkowsky asked, coming into their bedroom. She was bent over the battered night table, holding a postcard. "It's over a year old," Sara said, her cheeks turning a fiery pink, a color Milkowsky hadn't seen since they were teenagers. Handing it to him, his wife walked quickly into the living room as if in search of something, tapping her head.

The postcard was almost two years old. Later he deciphered this from the faint waving lines. It was the back of the card he read now. "Did you lose my number?" The digits were written out in the bold hand he remembered from the napkin. Under it a quotation: "In men who are hard, intimacy involves shame and is precious."

B.D. & F.N. was written at the bottom.

"I'm sorry," his wife called from the other room.

"It's okay. Nothing important. Just an old friend." But his

voice was quavering, it seemed to him, ringing hollow against
the bare walls and across the bleak, almost empty apartment.
He went on packing, but he and Sara avoided looking at each
other, and when Esther and Malkeh burst in with the youngest
in tow, Milkowsky called out that he was going down to the
office on Blue Hill to check some figures. The door slammed
behind him harder than he had intended, but he was too agi-
tated to turn back.

He was dressed in a pair of soiled pants and an old, torn
flannel shirt. Dust from the corners of the apartment from
which broken toys, books, and unusable articles had been retrieved streaked his cuffs and knees. There was a phone at the
corner of Harvard Street and Blue Hill, but he felt it was
cursed. In any event, he reasoned, he needed a walk, fresh air,
as the soot and dust kicked up by the packing had filled his
lungs. He struck out across the lawn of Franklin Field, skirting
the tennis courts and coming out on the opposite side before
he regained the thoroughfare.

It was cold and there were patches of snow from the night
before. Now it was melting, but in the snappy air Milkowsky
regretted that he had not brought a coat.

He felt an itch to put his head in The New Yorker and call
from there. "Betty must have married, moved away" rang
clearly in his head.

The phone was by the stairs that led down to the toilet and
near the swinging door of the kitchen—a difficult place to call
and be heard from, half public—but Milkowsky knew already
that there would be no answer.

"Hello?" The voice that spoke was familiar if slightly
faded. It was a man's.

"Is Betty Daugherty there?" Milkowsky asked.

"Who is this?" the familiar Irish lilt rang back.

"A friend," said Milkowsky.

"What sort of friend?"

"An old friend," Milkowsky answered.

"How old?" the canny brogue inquired.

Despite himself, Milkowsky laughed, his nervousness draining off in the crackling of the testy old man who interrogated him at the other end. It was the same number.

"About two years," Milkowsky volunteered.

"What's your name?"

"Jerry Milkowsky."

"Are you married?" the South Boston voice asked slowly and suspiciously.

"Are you her father?" Milkowsky countered.

"Yeah," the man admitted, taken aback by the quickness of his interlocutor.

"Is she there?" Milkowsky asked.

"She ain't been here for a year now."

"Can I get in touch with her?" Milkowsky went on.

"She calls sometimes," the voice confessed after a long pause. Milkowsky cut in briskly.

"Do you have an address?"

"Nope."

"Can you tell her I called?" The insurance salesman's request was delivered firmly.

"What's your name?" the girl's father asked.

Milkowsky spelled it out. He decided to leave his office number as well, adding, "Listen, Mr. Daugherty, when did you hear from her last?"

"Eight months ago."

"Well, I hope she calls."

"So do I." There was something very sad in the man's voice. "Are you a Jew?" he asked in the pause before Milkowsky was about to say thank you and hang up.

"Yes, I am. Why do you ask?"

"What do you do?" Betty's father asked.

"I sell insurance."

"That's okay. You're okay. Never mind. I'll tell her if she calls." Abruptly Milkowsky heard the phone being hung up on the other end.

A man was coming up from the squalid bathroom below, a cabby's hat cocked back on his head. His eyes focused on Milkowsky's in the yellow half-light of the stairway and sparked with a sudden sign of recognition in their green-and-gray reflection. A half smile pulled at the corners of the man's mouth. Putting his hand out to touch the soiled shirt of the figure who stood holding the dead receiver in his hand, the man said, "I *know* you. You're the guy . . ."

"I never saw you before." Milkowsky said it and raised his eyebrows, staring into the man's face. "But you better zip up your fly." He turned around, leaving the cabbie momentarily bewildered on the stairs, looking down at his pants.

Outside in the fresh air, though, Milkowsky suddenly wondered if he had lost his chance.

Under his tongue he tasted the radish. **Q**

SANDRA STONE

Dig and Delve

Because she was sitting at the table, her feet came right into the middle of his house. So he made them part of the house. He covered them up with the little blanket that was on the sofa, dragging it over and tucking it around her feet to hide them. But that did not look right, because her feet still stuck out. So he pulled the blanket back off and he untied her shoes. Then he tried to make her shoes come off. "Take your shoes off," he told her, but she did not answer. So he patted her shoes and thought they would fall off, her shoes, but they did not fall off. So he pulled on her shoelaces, but the shoes would not fall off. So he covered the shoes back up, but the toe of one of the shoes sticking out looked to him like the small nose of a small animal, so he patted the toe and tried to push the toe back in, but it would not go in. So he brought his bear and made the nose of the bear sniff at the toe of the shoe. Then he brought many more animals than Bear—three: Monkey and flop-eared Tucker and Gruff. And he looked all over for Grumble. When he asked Mrs. Young was Grumble in the washer, she said he wasn't. He didn't believe her, so he looked through the window of the door, but no. So he went back and he sat only the four of them, whatever way they sat, sagged down around her feet. Bear was the softest, because what had plumped him out had gone out of him. When he tried to make Bear sit up, he wouldn't. So he spanked Bear on the middle, but Bear wouldn't. So he made him lie down and take a nap. Then he made Monkey climb up the cushion, and Tucker be tuckered out at the foot of it, and Gruff stand at the crack in the cushion and guard it. Then he crawled out and brought some of the little ones that were fuzzy, and he rubbed them against his cheek. When he saw that she was watching him, he said, "Do you want me to do it to you?" And she smiled. So he reached up, but he could not reach her. So he tried to stand on the top of his toes, and he tried to make one of them do it to her, but it would not reach. Then she leaned down her cheek and he rubbed it on her cheek, letting the others fall down, and he made the right sounds, *cheep cheep cheep,* and then the wrong ones and laughed, and thought that it would make her laugh. But she only smiled. "Talk," he said, but she wouldn't. But when he was bringing the cushions over, she said, "What time is it?" So he looked at the clock, but he didn't know. So he went to Mrs. Young. She was shelling peas. She pulled on the top of them and bent them, and the peas fell out into the bowl on her lap. He said to her, "What time is it?"

Mrs. Young said, "What do you need to know for?"

And he said, carefully, "What time is it?"

She said, Mrs. Young said, "Eleven."

And he went back and told her, "Eleven." And then he thought about it, and after a while he said, "Twelve." And after he brought a cushion from the sofa, he said, "Dig and delve." Then he got his shovel and put it on the table next to her hand. She picked it up and looked at it. "It's new," he told her. Then he brought the little pot with the purple flower in it and put it on the table next to the shovel, and that was the dirt, but the flower was to smell, he smelled it to show her. She smiled. So he pushed it closer and it fell off the table. He worried that Mrs. Young would hear it, but no. So he took the shovel and made his hand into a cup on its side and he cupped the dirt onto the shovel. But the shovel was too big to go into the pot. So he took the dirt back off with the cup of his hand and sprinkled some of the dirt back into the pot. Some of the dirt fell onto the rug. It was a fluffy rug and he patted it in. He picked up one of the pebbles and put it back in the pot. "One, two," he said, and he took the pot with the purple flower in it and put it back on the windowsill.

"What time is it?" she said.

So he put down the next cushion that he was trying to make stand up and he went to ask Mrs. Young. She was stirring something. She had a big spoon. She had a little spoon that she was spilling something into the pot with. "Sh-hhh," she said, Mrs. Young said. So he had to ask her again and she said, the same as before, "Eleven."

"Again?" he said. He went back in the other room and told her. Then he got under the table and pulled the cushions in after him, *three, four,* so that just specks of light were in there with him, *shut the door.* And he put all the fuzzy ones between her shoes, *buckle my shoe,* and one of them sticking in the wheel of her chair, which he had not thought of before, *five, six.* So he stuck all of them in, *pick up sticks.* And he said all of their voices to them very softly in their house, where all of their sounds sounded to him like sounds far away. And he was just saying *growl* when he heard her voice. It sounded far away from the cave, the house where he was. The voice said, "What time is it?" And he did not want to go out from there, it was so warm and her feet so snug, so he said, "Eleven," and then, because he thought she would want to know, he said, "My mama is coming pretty soon." And he heard her say, "My mama is coming pretty soon, too." **Q**

A Hog Loves Its Life

[1] ONCE...

Language, like love, starts local.

My grandfather called me deep into the big house. We hid. While powdered aunts and freckled cousins yammered on his front porch—one old farmer scolded me. I was scared but liked it.

"Willy? Just heard you lipping-off to your mother—close to tantrum, you were. Keep doing that, you got no future. I won't have a grandson of mine carrying on like Lancaster's mule."

"Like *who*?"

This antique stared at me. (I might've asked if Jesus was the Father, Son, or Holy Ghost—if South Carolina didn't outrank our native North Carolina.)

"Like Lancaster's mule." First Grand doubted my hearing. When I still shrugged, he closed both eyes, pinched the bridge of his nose, and—sighing hard—motioned me up into his lap. The sigh smelled of medicine, baking soda, and leaf mold, of bread and years.

"Since 'wireless' came in, seems like nothing on this earth is *grounded.* My own flesh and blood especially. You sure don't know much. Where you *been,* boy?"

"I guess I'm young yet." This got me one respectful frown.

"Seems Lancaster dealt livestock. Boo-coo hogs and horses—that being French for 'heaps of.' (With you, son, I'm taking nothing for granted.) A jumbo size of a man, this Lancaster, all jaw was he, hair parted in the middle, the very middle. Animals were gods to us in the eighteen and nineties—and Buck, he *sold* them. Now, Willy, this I'm trying to tell you, it came previous to autocars, tractors, exhaust, all such mess. Maybe you think you're lucky being born so recent? Ha. Ha *ha*. More the fool you. You believe sputniks are worth writing home about? *Ha* ha. People wanted to get around the county in my time, people either bought something four-legged or else used good old shoe leather. Ever heard of it, you-in-all-the-car-pools? A person needed their field plowed, person either borrowed a hand hoe or got a good mule, one. As for Lancaster, his morals might've been the short end of nothing, but the man knew every confidence trick going, was just his nature to.

"Buck's been dead since '31. They all are. Most every-body's gone except your grandmother, wonderful woman, testy as she sometimes acts toward me. Last person alive knows to call me Little Bobby Grafton. Nowdays in this town, I'm held to be Mr. Grafton or Old-timer or Pops Grafton. But a body needs a few souls who remember he was Little Bobby Grafton, 'Ears,' the boy that lived in trouble. But wait, I'm wandering. One evening, closing time at Buck's stockyard, here comes a young hayseed. One born every minute—plenty to keep Buck busy and his daughters between satin sheets. 'You're seeking, don't tell me'—Lancaster touches one tem-ple—'an exceptional . . . mule.' The mouth-breathing farmer blinks, asks how Buck knew. 'Simple, son,' Buck says, 'little something we call genius. Ever heard of it? Follow me.' Which ends this part."

My teller paused, squaring his shoulders, primed. He talked the way binge drinkers, finally on vacation, drink. Bobby was considered tight-lipped. He saved his lurid best for me. I sat staring at the man.

Us grandkids called him Grand for short. He was semi-famous—the county white man with the record-largest ears. We are talking giant here. In those times in North Carolina, ears grew bigger. Especially farmers'. I studied cartilage sturdy as roofing shingles. Hinge-long, rust-colored—any hound could envy his. And I'd inherited the things. My mother wept about this. Literally wept. You can see how—all these years later—I've resisted having mine surgically subdued, a tribute.

"Willy? Buck did not know fear. Buck loved money the most. Buck was not exactly ugly—you can't call a bag of cement ugly—just there. Flashy dresser he was, though his linen pant cuffs tended to stay the color that a-man-who-owns-a-stockyard-and-wades-everywhere's pant cuffs will."

"Brown?"

"Now, as a mule salesman, Lancaster was known to fudge a bit. A bit! Did I say a bit?"

"Yes."

"Don't correct me here, Will. Because I won't sanction insolence. Not even from my best-looking grandchild. Boo-coo questions cannot be answered. Mine especially. Lancaster didn't fudge just some, oh no. He was a horse trader. You expected those to try and bilk you. Means 'cheat,' Willy. You went ready. I've always had a soft spot for the fellows can't resist but to drive a deal. I'm not so hot at it myself, pushover. Ask your grandmother, Ruth reminds me often enough. But Lancaster? Give such a gent fifteen hundred pounds of surplus steel wool, he'll knit you a hotel stove. Then he'll try and *sell* it to you. And, son, know what?"

"You'll buy it?" Grand squinted down at me, impressed with my quickness, bored by my character. "Willy? what'd I just tell you? *Just?*"

"Quiet?"

"Quiet. No wonder you know jack-nothing—way you keep busting in on a person. Look, do you want this or not? Ask me for it."

"I do."

"Do what?"

"Want. I'll keep still. I promise. It's just . . . I . . ."

"You're goddamn right you will. Should've seen *me* back then. One thing sure, could've beat *you* up, both hands tied behind me. Scrappy. We had to be."

"But, Grand, know what? I bet I'm probably smarter."

Inner corners of forty wrinkles tightened, that ashamed: a boy had admitted that another boy might trounce him.

"I didn't hear that. Buck Lancaster owned a fine three-story house, had four overly average-looking daughters. Sundays you'd ride by, Buck's girls'd be lined up along his porch, one softer than her baby sister. Did I say, 'You'd *ride* by . . .'?"

(This time—a quick study—I knew to say nothing.)

"More like walk by. Our farm was five miles out, just where they're putting in the shopping mall. Willy? I don't want it to go there. Driving past it makes me vomit. Fact, son. I see them chopping up our north pasture, jabbing stakes everywhere, I pull my Packard to the side of the road, I sacrifice whatever excellent lunch Ruth fed me. I do. My momma's stand of hollyhocks grew right in that field, still coming up last spring. Hollyhocks aren't supposed to bloom your first year—like asparagus, you only expect yields the second. Hers bloomed year number one and quite a clump, pink. Rare enough so people buggied out to see.

"But back then, in the real time, I hiked to town wearing my one Sunday suit. Faked errands all over a neighborhood where not a soul knew me, was studying Lancaster's beauty girls in pastel dresses. 'Ears' was all eyes then, boy. To and fro went Little Bobby Grafton, the boy that lived in trouble, hoping to get into a better class of Bobby trouble than Bobby's usual. You think those girls couldn't guess who I was staring at! Ha. I might not've been as quick as you in a *book* way—with Poppa snatching me out of Lower Normal every time something got ripe enough to pick or cut—but I could've told you to Shut Up and you would've.

"Lancaster's girls had a parrot on the porch with them. A parrot in this town then, it really meant something. Showed sparrows weren't the half of it. And not one Lancaster girl ever married—is how hard a bargain Buck drove. No governor was fat, rosy, or rich enough to get in good with *Buck's* girls.

"So anyhow, the mule of it—along around closing time, near sunset on a slow week night, barn swallows probably went skimming over tin roofs (though I couldn't swear to it), into Buck's drags that same slow-moving young farmer from out Pitt County way. (Your grandmother was a Pitt and she will tell you in a minute if you don't stop her. Pretty much a snob, but she sometimes seems to fancy me—so I can't find total fault with her.) Young fellow craved a serious working mule. Buck just happened to have one. Office was already padlocked, but Buck could smell a pocketful of bills, damp from this plowboy's clutching them clear to town. So Buck swings into his friendliest style, hands our dirt farmer one fine cigar—the first that boy'd ever had, I bet you. Just to get a fellow's *con*fidence, don't you know. Leads our boy around back where not one streetlamp burns. And here in a dark corral stands the matted-eyed knock-kneed mule, all by its lonesome and acting real homesick for *some*thing.

"Lancaster might have said, 'Stranger, you are doubtless wondering—clever operator such as yourself—why I chose to separate this creature from its own born kind.' Buck talked like that, only way worse. Trust me to talk like they talked. To try. Now we're getting near the real part, part where I come in. Now we're near knee-deep in it." And gazing before him, Grand literally rubbed his leather palms together.

The rest of our family still jabbered on the bright porch. Jaw jaw jaw, gas gas gas. A waste. Out front—my grandmother's clear tone straddled three conversations, governing them. Family talk sounded like one church organ's many pipes and tubes—flute- to chimney-sized—all alive with a single feeding breath.

I worried: my weight might be hurting Grand's arthritis. But in Falls, N.C. in 1962—if you were ten years old, grandfathers invited you up onto their laps, even if it really pained them. They practically had to, some grandfatherly union regulation. Grand's easy chair was a huge orange leatherette slab. He'd bought it at some cut-rate store; its ugliness daily grieved my grandmother. The matching footstool steadily leaked sawdust onto her inherited Aubusson carpet. "It molts," she said.

I watched narrow lips move, silent, as Grand carpentered our next part. He studied air directly before his face. He was one of those people that, like a dog or mule, lets you stare. They hardly notice till—with you an inch away, your saying "Hey" can make them jump like something shot. This man owned four stores, ten rental homes, and the most broken-down dirt farm you ever saw. I admired how much property he'd piled up from total scratch. Little Bobby Grafton's folks had mostly worked as sharecroppers, their lives spent improving others' fields. As a day-labor kid, Grand got sun-cooked across his neck and over both hands' leathery backs (*roofs* of his hands, I considered them). His skin seemed lidded like the old-timey thick-topped butterscotch pudding my grand-mother served. She called this favorite dessert "commonplace but comforting." His was the face of a small-time landowner—accustomed to squinting with slit-eyed pride at mortgaged horizons. During summer, when he gimped in from a burning day outdoors, his stately wife met him on the porch. She held a jar of Nivea, as blue as the future. "Sun seems to consider these poor ears perfect targets." Ruth stationed herself behind his chair; she removed her ruby ring, slathered up either hand and, focusing on the mammoth flanges, started daubing.

(Whenever *my* first wife feared losing one of our arguments, she hinted I should go and have my ears surgically "pinned." Hideous word, "pinned"—especially when the features are yours and visibly inherited. I had confided Grand's early nickname: "Bi-plane Grafton." And do you know she used this against me, in front of two other couples and in a good New York restaurant? She did. She hinted we were presently getting such poor service because of a certain rustic somebody's ear size. "Obscene," she once called these units you've occasionally glanced at. Go ahead—hey, no offense, really. My first wife's inappropriateness finally stuck out even more than do these Willy flaps. They're still with me, she is not.)

"Now—buddy-ro for which I'm trying to spell what 'like

Lancaster's mule' means, young as you are, and as lost in the modern world as everybody seems now, do *you* figure it's too good of an idea, buying yourself a mule—or, for that matter, a little runabout motorcar—at nighttime? Huh, Willy? I'm asking this one straight out, so go ahead and answer if you can.''

I stalled. With Grand, I kept my favored standing by avoiding the porch (its gossip was considered beaucoup more entertaining than his). He loved my admitting what I didn't know, he loved the way I pleaded for his Sunday installments. He let me take out his pocketwatch and fidget with its chain's three toy brass horseshoes (they came with penny candy in the 1890s, when animals were still the gauge of distances and dollars). But if Grand offered me direct questions, I could not be wrong twice in a single visit. My mother explained I need not humor the old man. She considered her father-in-law sweet, well-meaning, reasonably pathetic. While I sat indoors with him, I missed some good porch rumors, ones my folks and kid brothers would mention in our station wagon bound home to the suburbs. But I was hooked on his fierce attention, on weekly news from one gent literally rednecked. Sundays I rushed toward his chair. "Okay, start me off with 'Carlton's Wren,' then do 'Lessie Poland's Boot,' the long way. I mean, please, sir, *please* do those ones first.''

Mention any creek from Pitt to Nash Counties, you'd siphon a tale. The awful flood of '89; the beautiful sisters who left a note, then drowned on purpose; the fellow who swapped Indian Creek for a diamond brooch, then lost it to his wife at poker. When our station wagon zoomed home from Grand's and over a bridge, I looked down on Legend. My loved ones saw just weeds and bilge.

Our *Compton's Encyclopedia* showed Egyptian murals: Pharaohs were giant athletes—their helpful midget commoners came knee-high. For Grand, the dead of Falls were royally huge. They towered over all us present pygmies of the 1950s. (Ours was an age of sleekest tail fins. A big war had just been won; Falls's stores sold smooth, good, streamlined things.

Each year at the State Fair, we saw U.S. Army rockets displayed, but mules?—they were already so scarce in suburban Falls. If some hold-out farmer led one down our street, people swarmed outdoors, smiling, aiming Kodaks, calling, "You kids? unglue yourself from that TV set. Come look for once. You'll thank me later. It's historical.")

My own secret interest in the future changed how I heard Grand's yarns. He weekly binged forth a gallery of good-sized hucksters—men brilliant as my *Superman* comics' space masterminds. At ten, I was a glum little comic-book pedant (such kids are now computer whizzes). I listened to the muddy landscape Grand described, but sent it light-years forward into chilly mineral space. I pictured crystal tower residences so tall, spotlights shone up top warning away rocket ships. Grand often mentioned hogs; I reshaped even these: rooting carnivorous robot units, stainless steel as Mother's weekday flatware. Here and now, alive and in secret in modern life, I'd found a talking map. He stayed hushed around others, semi-dignified; but with me in lap, Grand sketched a space frontier: vigilantes, potent animals, robberies, feuds. His past unrolled a fresh (free) Marvel Comic series. Soon, our own Indian Creek—wagered for diamonds, lost at cards—seemed mythic as some Mars canal traded for hunks of white-hot, Kryptonite.

Grand's mission? explaining Falls's deceased to Falls's more newly born.—Who new cared except his single scrawny disciple, the one kid willing to stay indoors, to shut up for a change, and just sit here big-eyed, positively floppy with hearing equipment? The old man told and told—unaware of giving me a future, not a past.

I finally risked: "No, sir. It's not really all that good of an idea, buying stuff at night and everything. Because, see? it's dark and they could . . . put something over on you."

Which got me one raw assessing look. Praise might be hid in it; I couldn't yet decide. So, taking a chance, I added, "Lancaster especially."

A shudder ran through runty knobbled shoulders. Grand stared. For a second I feared I needed to blow my nose, so rarely did he gape right at a person's face. Then hard hands slipped under my arms, he turned me (roughly) toward window light, he checked my freckles—coded like star charts or our genes. "I know whose grandchild *this* one is. Folks, how *about* our Willy here?" But looking around the parlor, Grand found everybody'd wandered to the airier front porch. Even so, he held me inches up in air, showing me off to absolutely nothing. " 'Lancaster especially,' says this one, like he was there. I like that. 'Lancaster *espec*ially.' " He set me down harder and sooner than I wanted.

"So Buck says to our farmer, says, 'Sir, what you're studying is the smartest single mule currently alive in our continental America, meaning, fellow patriot, the world generally. Please greet the Mule of Your Dreams, why, the mule of *anybody's*. But first tell me how you heard about him. You waited till closing time when all the earlier bidders got dragged away, right, you dog, you?' Buck was not above nudging a fellow's ribs. Whatever works. The poor farmer grinned—sucker was slow, Willy. I've heard your mother talk about somebody's children having reading problems and all like that. There is— your present-day liberal hates admitting—such a thing as plain D.V.M. And this clodhopper *was* it. What can you do?

"Goes Buck, 'Certain mules kept torturing this paragon, actually biting him. I'm ashamed to admit: some kicking was involved. So we hid our rarity. Reason? I caught him trying to plow, sir. Kept digging ruts, using nothing but his hoof. At the time, it was all he had *on* him. Pulling said hoof back and forth, making little furrows, steady as a Singer. By noon, my front paddock could have been the start of a decent truck garden. Of course, the other mules hate this one for being so work-loving. So here it is, banished from its shiftless kind, the work-ingest damn animule I have laid eyes on in my fifty years of community service from one single convenient location.' Buck adds that if all this is not true, may his lovely daughters suffer chilblains, gout, and facial warts right . . . this . . . *sec*-ond. He stands still, like listening. One slow grin proves honesty's won out again, his girls are yet smooth as satin sheets. Buck tells the customer to go freely peruse yonder mule. But our farmer cannot get a real clear look-see, and why, Willy?"

"It's still night."

"You're goddamn right, it's still night. And by now it's pitch-black coal-bin midnight dark. Lancaster's moving faster. 'Young sir, I love dealing with gents who so *know* mulekind. Heck, *let* those other bidders duke it out come morning. For a price, our dream mule here is yours alone.' Now, say the beast cost eighty dollars. Might sound cheap to a pip with an allowance big as yours (your daddy told me what he pays you for doing nothing). But back then, money was still a law unto itself. Why, you could get you a whole motorcar for under three hundred dollars, new."

"Naw." I slapped the leather roof of his hand. "Naw. *New?*" (I pictured a rocket ship, all my own and as silver as Reynolds Wrap.)

"Truth. Sure. Brand-new. Tires inclusive. (Means: it comes *with*, Will.) So that farmer'd shelled out his whole life savings. Boo-coo bucks. And don't you know, his wife and kids were waiting up by lantern light to see what hero-animal they'd got. Maybe they patted it, probably they named it. We named everything back then. My daddy's favorite plow was called Atlas . . . be one example. I still know the names of certain hogs I personally ate most of. I'm saying this to feed the fire of our story till I tiptoe in with what I eyewitness-saw. Plus I'm hoping to put off going out on the porch, having your grandmother tell me in front of everybody that I'm wearing one too many plaids again—how do people know? Come dawn, our poor farmer was probably up before the larks—if we *had* any round these parts, well, meadowlarks, I guess we do—he hit a snag once the harness was oiled, plow-sharpened, ready to start life over behind the Mule of His Dreams—behind the mule of anybody's, Willy o' mine . . ."

(Since I turned four, Grand had ignored my faintly-suburban first name. "Bryan is somebody's *last* name. And not *ours* either. No, here we got a person called Willy . . . it's as solid of a Willy as I've ever seen." Since then I have tried becoming the pure shrewd decent country "Willy" Grand considered me. Even in my present spreading urban middle age, I work at being worthy of the name.)

"Now we finally strike my own patch of it, a relief. Good clean fun, Buck's hog sales. Free. What us poor kids had instead of wireless or these new television sets. Maybe I was only your age and yea-high to nothing, but 'Ears' Grafton was all-eyeballs in the front row. Here comes Little Bobby Grafton who lived in trouble and missed nothing and got punished even for things he didn't do, but never snitched on who did. A boy like you, only maybe keener, if not so book-smart. Your daddy went to Harvard College—though *I* paid for it. He swears you will. Go there. *He'll* have to pay. I don't know as I approve. Your dad's still rotten with Cambridge this and that. If you go, you'll probably forget everything Grand here ever tried telling. But I plan to anyhow. Nobody can say *my* Willy never learned what 'Lancaster's mule' means. Sure I was scrappier and smarter than you are now—but not by much, so don't pout so.

"Was the morning after last night's mule sale, was during a hog auction, with Buck conducting bidding at forty miles a minute (who *else* would he trust to do it?). Say Buck was making regular waltz music and a sermon from his morning's shoat sale, when in blunders our young hayseed. Boy's definitely gnawing his lower lip, dark in the face, hat pulled low, leading the selfsame mule (all dusty now, limping bad, one eye closed). The farmer also totes a huge aught-aught shotgun, old-fashioned even for then. Quite the hush falls over everything, hogs included. Hogs are smart, Will. A hog loves its life.

"Soon as Buck spots that musket, which just *looks* loaded, he signals everybody to please hold still, not run for cover. Not yet. Using eyebrows only, he hints how his hirelings should sneak behind the customer, disarm him. And you can wager that during all of this, Buck kept the last and highest hog bid in his head. Didn't his very *name* have a 'Buck' in it? He grins. 'So, my agriculturally-minded young friend, returned to the scene of earlier glories, I see. What, sir, can we do for you today?'

"At this the farmer gets to breathing funnier, hiccuping, little stray burps roll out—uncontrolled, we're talking here. 'What can *you* do? What can you *do*?' his red face under the straw brim goes toward purple. "More like *un*do, you double-dipping jackal. You might could give me my durn money back with interest and travel expenses. Is one thing you might could do. To save your hide. I'm here to announce before every other fool present, Mr. Lancaster, that me, my precious wife and six children—we consider you a . . . flesh-eating liar and a thief.'

"Certain murmuring rises. Even hogs squeal some, like whistling. A hog knows a insult when he hears it; a hog is so smart that he can . . . Hogs are smart. But not *that* smart, Will. What is it about you makes me tack on extra stuff?

" 'Those'—Lancaster stands taller—'constitute strong words, stranger.' (He's secretly signing his hog gaffers to sneak up from behind.) Meantime, Lancaster stalls by checking his famous pocketwatch. The case chimes open, its usual hymn 'Work for the Night Is Coming.' Buck rolls eyes through barn roof and heavenward.

"Hirelings whip off their hats to prove how religious Buck is. Lancaster does a silent 'Amen,' grinning down the gun's very barrel. 'Come, let us reason together. As says the Book. Take it you had a bit of trouble managing your new animal?'

" 'Trouble? Trou-ble? Mr. Snake, I'm up before sunrise, planning to get a full day's work from this critter I paid way too dear for. Broke out the new harness. Even combed my *own* hair. Overdid, I admit it. My wife and young ones line along our fence, smiling, half asleep. Well, our noise wakes the new mule. Seems a good sign. He trots out of the barn. He takes him a deep breath. Well, that strikes us *all* as a pretty good sign. A lot of nodding from folks on the fence to me, from me back to them at the fence, then back to . . .'

" 'Get *on* with it,' Buck snaps, bold—even at gunpoint. That Buck! We should all be more like him.

" 'My new mule breaks into a full trot (extra good sign). Mule heads straight toward the only oak tree in my paddock. Mule knocks hisself clean out. Lays there, cold-cocked, panting in the dust. Well, me and my family eyeball each other. Mule finally comes around, shakes his head, picks hisself up, leans on the tree for help. I'm thinking: Could happen to *any* creature, just overeager is all. Pounds into the side of my barn. Hits so hard—half the hay I spent all Saturday getting up there drops. Not real good of a sign. Every time he came to, got his bearings, he'd gallop slap into some fence, wagon, barn, tree, barn, barn, tree, fence. *Lancaster*—I don't mind telling you and all these fellow suckers, my wife and babies just stood at our fence crying. They acted disappointed in my *judg*ment. And I'm man enough to admit: made me cry, too. So, you latrine-mouthed coyote—I am here to get a total refund or your life, one. Because, Lancaster, you done went and sold me a blind mule!'

"Now, Willy, Lancaster rocks back on his heels, sizes up the moment like it is for sale. 'My good man,' Lancaster says, thumbs crooked into vest pockets, watch chain dangling, and him staring out at the auction crowd, getting folks ready. *'My good man, that mule ain't blind. That mule just don't give a damn.'*

"Well, everybody fell out. In such hooting, somebody yanked the rifle off the unhappy customer. Buck offered him a new seeing-eye mule, plus let him keep the other one. But the poor fellows's Pitt County reputation was ruined, permanent, because he'd tried to buy a mule . . . help me out here, Willy, who from?"

"Lancaster especially!"

"And at when . . . ?"

"At pitch-black dark night!" My eyes nearly popped, that

cooperative with the story. I breathed deeper, as if we'd just come a great distance at a hard gallop, which we had.

"Why, I should say *so.* Anyhow, from that very minute forward, all around here for three counties easy, folks just fell in love with saying that. Found it . . . useful, as a story. And ever since, whenever people my age and your daddy's speak of anybody doing crazy and being wild and trying whatever strikes them and not *minding* banging their heads against whatever's in the way—well, we call them what, Willy?"

Solemn, I answered.

"And odd part, even though that poor mule *was* blind— what caught on was Lancaster's turning its being blind into a joke that saved his neck. So, see, Will, a good story, if it comes at just the right second, adds up to something. Slips into folks' everyday talk. And this whole one I've told—to keep you from ending up crazy-mean and by your lonesome, plus because you're young yet and have missed so much good stuff that came before you, stuff that surely won't strike ever again—it all stays crated up forever in those four words."

Silently I practiced.

"Moral being today—you'd best straighten up and do right or you'll quit being *my* pick of the litter. Plus, nobody'll ever come near you. Willy? you don't want to end up corraled all *alone,* do you, son?"

I wagged my head NO, SIR. I turned then—my back fitted against Grand's front. I shifted my weight to his opposite hipbone. That way, maybe I wouldn't hurt one arthritis place so much. Speckled arms locked around me matter-of-factly. The chair wheezed. We both seemed heavier now his tale was done. Sawdust probably trickled onto Grandmother's inherited rug—an hourglass-spill running straight out of us. From the porch: voices of women/men (political fighting), bickering grandkids (contested toys).

One of my heavier aunts now bounded past our chair, rushing toward the bathroom. (She always waited till the last moment—afraid she'd miss something good—then she had to gallop. Family joke—one of many.) "Oh," Auntie said, startled. "Oh, you all. It's *chilly* in here. I don't know why you don't come outside like *soc*iable people." I planned scoffing at her when I heard Grand, asleep already. Farm sinew thrummed two, short questioning snores. To avoid talking back to Auntie or apologizing, I shut my eyes (an old man's trick).

The bathroom door double-locked. One uncle outside laughed. "Says who? Where's that law written?" Shocking, how many others still jabbered out there, ignorant, unsteady, too up-to-date. Poor pygmies-of-the-present—offered nothing but shrinking crawl space. The future alone would allow us decent headroom. Thanks to vitamins and rocket travel, we'd be bigger-headed but heroic. Each our own car pool, flying out safe in front.

From my throne within a farmer's ropy arms, I found I really pitied the weak, the living. Our Dead were giants who'd done battle. The last word stayed theirs. Grand had filled me up with them. My gossip was the gossip of the dead. At ten, I saw it as prediction. At ten, I still believed in the future.

This shadowed house felt cool and blue, full of ticking clocks I hadn't noticed while he talked. Ten Swiss mantel clocks—wound every single American Monday morning since 1911. A front porch blazed, iced-tea glasses clinked. Another endless sneezy summer afternoon.

Grand breathed beneath me. He seemed to breathe for me. I thought, Us two, we've just picked to be dis*guised* as earthlings a while, see.

Earthlings for now. I nodded, sleepy. My ambitious ears lightly touched Grand's cotton shirt sleeves. His front felt spongy, gigantic underneath me. Mulch and trampoline—my past.

Auntie finally prissed back by us, then turned—tugging at her hemline, centering her belt. She'd smudged on lipstick. As I watched with one eye, she gummed red marks onto a doubled Kleenex, then studied her own mouth-track. She read it like some love note from the future. "So [blot] which one's he been [blot] trying to tell you today, Bryan? He always exaggerates, honey, don't you believe a third of what he says." My eyes pressed shut so tight they quivered. Then Grand and me were left alone, somehow more male for the interruption.

His chair was orange and under him—ugly, comfortable. He was mottled pink and orange and under me. He was a crank. I was a crank in training. He was shy around others. He saved his best for me. He had big ears. I had huge ears, grand ones.

And I believed the man: I'd better straighten up, fly right. Otherwise I might get stuck alone in some future cold-as-space. (Boy, what a waste *that'd* be, especially considering my straight-A record and how basically nice I was!) I practiced mumbling the new term many different ways. It'd prove useful up ahead. "The future" would be lots better than just "later on." Wouldn't it? I now reached down, I touched the roof of one cracked hand.

In 1962, I didn't know: the future would do *any*thing. I whispered, "Crazy as Lancaster's mule."

[2] EVENTUALLY...

The old man enjoyed few great local successes. He prospered in a small-time way. Little Bobby Grafton was the hero of no story but my own, which this partly is. I found his tales entertaining till I turned thirteen, suddenly too old for them, for him. His favorites always featured other slickers in the leading roles. Maybe my grandmother's fondest stories put her Bobby front and center. She's dead, of course. But I'm not.

Grand was a steady, half-religious, usually quiet fellow, a major buyer of Kiwanis Club peanuts and Brooms by the Blind. He let himself be dragged to church on Christmas and Easter only. He was a great one for crime magazines and subscribed to three. Bobby considered these superb bathroom reading. My grandmother bought chintz book covers to improve his latest "numbers."

Grand stayed one of those tender sideline small-town guys who're always there when it happens, expert witness to others' triumphs. "Hey, Bobby? Come over here and tell these people how I told off that rude waitress that time, remember?" And he would: he'd block it out at his own farming pace, promoting the cad to a regular hero. People loved "Ears" Grafton for his skill at making them look bigger.

Though ridiculously and unprofitably honest himself, he admired the scams of strangers. He collected lore concerning folks who walk to the corner store for a newspaper and are never seen again and who've embezzled millions. "Untold millions," I once heard him dreamily say. In 1962, Grand drove as far as Cary, North Carolina, just to see a Wachovia bank that'd been held up the previous Friday. He spoke about one bullet hole in a plate-glass door; he mentioned it so often that Ruth, his dignified wife, took to screaming and covering her ears and running from the room. A mild person, he had lent cash to many souls in town. Who soon forgot. Bobby hated cruelty but loved pure nerve. In others. From behind his *Raleigh News and Observer,* he would chuckle, "That Mickey-the-Mouse-Mask robber has sure pulled a good one *this* time. Listen up, honey."

My grandmother's gall was just the kind that Little Bobby admired.

The august former Ruth Eder Pitt was ingenious as any Buck Lancaster, though fitted for more genteel purposes. She was a finely made woman with big incongruous jolly breasts. Her hair must've been nearly four feet long come morning before she again wove it against her head—tight as a beautiful basket you might buy. Bobby could sit all day on the porch rereading back-issue *True Detective;* Bobby entertained chums who stopped to hear enlarged versions of their own tired early exploits. "Yeah." They smiled. "I guess I *was,* I guess I *did*."

Ruth interrupted, aiming Bobby toward whatever profit he

ever earned. The young Miss Pitt, in 1901, enjoyed some
money of her own. She forever after called this "Bobby's seed
money." She mentioned it fairly often. She saw her nest egg
gained or lost in Grafton's every business deal. (My family's
recent joke about our Ruth: "She was from *the* Pitts.")

When I was ten, Grand still owned six rental homes on a
street nobody would choose but where many lived anyway.
Bobby collected the rent himself. "Only seems fair." If a
tenant's excuse for this month's lack of cash got stated in
a vivid, well-told tale, Grand might just let him slide. For a
month or three.

"Mr. Grafton, sir, you're never going to believe this but I
swear it on a stack of Bibles; if you don't trust me, ask my
Wanda (Wanda, haul your sweet carcass out here, sugar). My
foreman down to the mill has got it *in* for me. Just does.
Large-boned fellow, sir, and on Thursday—was it Thursday,
Wanda? so I suspected—in he comes big as life, one serious
grudging look in his eye, that if looks could kill—and they *can,*
Mr. G., for a person half as sensitive as I unfortunately am—
bring the coffee, Wanda, bit of white-lightning sweetener in
that for you, Mr. G.? So here my foreman comes, saying, 'I just
hate your *face,* son,' at which point I, being a proud man—
poor, sir, but proud—just *had* to carry that sledgehammer out
toward his fancy new Studebaker. Well . . . so then things sure
heated up quick . . ."

Grand leased two corner groceries in Falls's black district.
Few black merchants then sold on long-term credit. But at
stores Grand owned, if some debtor happened to be on hand
the day Mr. Grafton arrived (folks hung around like attending
some audition)—and if the debtor could then play a handy
blues guitar for the boss man and his best-looking grandson—
breaking an Orange Crush bottle against a nearby brick and
using its neck to mute and sift sounds till you heard a train
whistle getting nearer—and at night!—well, that man's bill was
permitted to coast for another little while.

When Grand drove his black Packard home from some

rent-collecting trip, arriving empty-handed (except for a string of gamey sunfish, one new tune, and three excellent almost-new hard-luck stories), his bosomy, beautifully appointed wife stood waiting by the front door. "Where *is* it?" Ruth held out her hand. She belonged to that generation where the wife was often depicted clasping her single weapon—a rolling pin. I haven't *seen* a rolling pin since 1960.

Ruth said, "It's like slave days for Little Bobby Grafton here. Only without anybody's being required to actually work for us. Slave owners fed their slaves—and that part he remembers. Meanwhile, we can't even get the front yard mown, and here he is off feeding and clothing half of our Negro community just for the pleasure of their charming excuses. I've never seen anything like it. If it weren't for my poppa's money, we'd have long since been dragged di*rec*tly to the poorhouse."

(Grand once told me, top secret, the full inventory of Ruth's 1901 dowry: a good rawhide suitcase, the French rug, two pig-iron bedsteads, a fifty-dollar gold piece, one ruby-chip ring, a couple of cloisonné lamps and flower vases, plus the monogrammed linens. Period.)

Grandmother often mentioned her husband's way with clothes: "It's not so much poor taste. Bobby has *un*-taste. I can send him to the finest store in driving distance, one you'd think has stocked nothing but charcoal gray for thirty-five years. But he'll *make* them go to the cellar—force them, beguile them, you know how he is—and they'll scare up some houndstooth horse-blanket thing—a mat, I won't call it a coat, it was a sort of *mat* with armholes. He comes to the car holding the thing, and I promise this: *you can see it through the paper bag.* Admit it, Bobby. Tell them. It's still in one of the closets in the guest room. Go get it, Bobby. Show them. Admit you chose it. If it's not upstairs, that's because I sent it to the vet's and had it put down. Which would, I daresay, be the only way you could get it out of the house and prevent its actually baying at a full moon! Or something. You see, now he's got *me* sounding like him. I won't have it, do you *hear* me, Little Bobby? I just won't, sir. *You* over there, wipe that smirk off those ears, hear?"

When he left for work, Ruth daily scanned him by their front door. She often ordered him—looking down at himself, huffing, mystified—right back up to his room, to change, this very instant.

Ruth and Bobby—en route to Florida by car in 1949—stopped at a tourist camp. Around 4 A.M., they smelled smoke, sat up to find the motel mostly on fire. A stunning wordless teamwork took over as she ran left, he adrenalined right—as they pounded and kicked on each door, waking every guest. Only later, by the glow of flames, by the fire trucks' raking red lights, did others (then my grandparents) slowly recognize: one old ribby gent and his bosomy partner were and had been totally naked all during. Bobby grinned. "Well, what do you know?" Blankets embroidered with the motel name settled over himself, his wife—a Pitt and therefore unperturbed by flames, strangers, frontal nudity.

Unusual for their generation, these two slept bare-assed and bragged about it. When, years later, Ruth got rushed to the hospital, her daughters-in-law ransacked dresser drawers, then phoned the best store in town, ordering what might've been the old woman's first nightie ever—ivory-colored satin worthy of a bride. "Romeo and Juliet," my father said of his own parents; but under his irony ran an envy we all felt—even the kids did.

My parents hated Grand's calling their Bryan "Willy." Ruth shamed Grand for it. "People will think you don't *know* better, Little Bobby, and him your own flesh and blood." She considered this a possible first hint of galloping senility. She seemed to revel in Grand's early memory goofs. "I'm afraid you're really slipping now. What shall we *do* with you?" and she touched his splotchy hand. Mentioning her husband's several faults, Ruth would corner anybody, black or white, friend or stranger. He sat right there all during, sat still and smily.

Little Bobby looked up at her—raucous with squint-eyed love as she admitted his frequent lapses. Ruth claimed he'd once owned every fashionable section of Falls, till roughly two months before it *became* fashionable, at which point he sold it at a dreadful loss. "Didn't you?" A gentle blinking nod. "Also, what's far worse, I fear—you all see that gentleman over there, the one with the exceptional hearing? in 19 and 19 he went and peddled our 650 shares of Coca-Cola stock for something like a dollar forty per share. Now, *did*n't you, Bobby? Fess up and get this part over with," and she wandered to his chair, brushed white hair off his forehead. He nodded, grinning, scratching at sunburned cartilage. "Ruth, honey? Believe it was—dollar *ten* a share."

I am thirty-nine years old. (I can't accept how aged I've become. My mother, who'll turn seventy this May, is glad (since misery loves company)—my ex-wives are probably unsurprised and might consider my being upset as just more typical vanity. Only *I* feel stunned and lonely, hearing the Niagara of forty roaring just ahead.) Now, in trying to recall the few perfect couples I have known, my grandparents seem about the most contented. At best, it's a fairly short list. Around 12:15 A.M., after an evening of whining about our love lives, my friends sometimes say, "Well, who-married do we even *know* that's really happy?"

"Now, when you say 'happy,' how do you mean it? I guess you mean . . . ?"

"Happy. Just really *hap*py, ever heard of it? . . . It used to be a concept."

My grandfolks were. What they mostly did: buttonhole anybody nearby—service-station men, hotel maids, family—and bad-mouth one another.

He called her a Gibson girl debutante run to seed; she said he was the most shiftless thing still half alive. And all during, they aimed sleepy, narrowed smiles at one another. I know it's now unfashionable, one person saying, "I own you and you own me." But I swear, theirs was the curt dreamy look of sovereign ownership. Maybe such love can occur only during the heyday of a rustic capitalist society.

In their household crowded with kin, you'd see the pair retreat to some corner, conferring about supper. Speaking, faces hovering unsentimental inches apart—one of them would idly lift a white hair off the other's gray-worsted shoulder; next, a straightening of the other's overbright tie. Soon their fingers were all over each other, efficient. Watching, you understood: they didn't even *know* they were in contact. If you pointed this out, they would loudly deny it. After sixty years of married days, their separate bodies had become that mutual, that pooled. Fondest strokings always started as sharpest criticism.

"Just *look* at you," she'd say, he'd say.

Ruth died before he did. I can tell you, she never meant to. Among the few wishes Ruth Eder Pitt Grafton was not granted: outliving Little Bobby. I once heard the woman, alone in the kitchen, cutting a first large piece of cake for him, explaining to no one, "Should anything ever happen to *me* . . ." Many spouses say this. We heard her but never quite believed till later.

The day before Ruth died, Grand drove a Packard-load of grandkids to the hospital. Nobody under twelve was allowed to visit. Our grandfather led us up a fire-exit side entrance— pausing for breath on each landing. Grand quietly told us he would take the full official blame. We just had to see her a last time. If the rules aren't fair—he said—if there's no time left to change the rules, a person broke them, a person had to.

I was twelve, the oldest kid present. (I later discovered that many of Bobby's grandkids felt *they* were his all-time secret favorite. This actually upset me briefly, but I still believe I was and am.) The batch of us—ages five to twelve—kept silent for a change. A hospital stairwell echoes so. I remember somebody's terry-cloth slipper (one only) was resting on a landing. It had three drops of blood across its top, like a design. "Yisch," my youngest girl cousin whispered, prodding it with the toe of her blue Ked.

We were herded toward a doorway. We felt pretty nervous at maybe being caught on the third floor, nervous about seeing Grandmother. It would be our very first viewing of Mrs. Ruth—our lifetime hostess—as somebody out of control. I stood in her half-open doorway surrounded by curly blond younger cousins, mostly girls. I felt scared by this hall's alcohol smell, by two different kinds of serious coughing nearby. I dreaded stepping into the room but felt I couldn't hold back now and disappoint Bobby Grafton.

She looked strangely small in a large, high bed. I'd never seen her with her hair unbraided. It uncoiled long as a witch's and—though I hated myself—to me it looked obscene all over the pillows like that. No discipline.

Even then, modern medicine was working those miracles that jab tubes into every outlet of the dying. Such help renders departing souls just conscious enough to be aware of this foreground indignity, it annoys them just enough to distract from Last Things. Right in my wallet here I've got a card telling authorities to withhold any such assistance from me, thank you. I'm not yet forty but have learned from my poor loved ones' polluted exits.

"Come in," Grand called. I really didn't want to step into that room. I saw clear hanging sacks and tubing. But I was scared that, if I didn't cross the threshold, my little cousins might mutiny, turn back. So, dutiful, I took a breath, I stepped right in. I have always been dutiful. It is the thing about myself I really hate the most. It is the thing about myself I love almost the most. How do you figure it?

Grand wanted us to see this woman dying. Another form of storytelling, showing her now—Bobby, born middleman at other people's dramas. This happened in winter. The heating system beat throughout the ward. One radiator against her room's far wall now rocked in place, clanging like a metal seizure chained up near the bed. I stood, my thin arms drooped over the shoulders of plump little cousins gathered against, around, below me. "Uck," one whispered. "What'd they *do* to her? *That's* not her."

"Come closer." The old man waved, smiling from the bed. "Ruth's hair, look, her hair has always been this long. So fine. Brown when I met her. It got blonder before turning silver, then white, like it is now. Happened in less than six months. There's still a lot of brown in it if you know what color to look for. Started out the shade of clover honey. Look at her. Come on in, do." Our group's spoiled youngest just said, "No." She stomped one foot, she wouldn't budge.

Some kids had edged nearer the bed, most remained half huddled in the hall, holding on to the doorjamb as if the sight of our grandmother might make a great gust that'd blow us all back down the stairs. Nurses began noticing us here. Nurses didn't want to be bothered. They'd surely seen other grand-children file into the hall for other enforced death watches. To keep officials from trudging down here and complaining, I must now get my cousins into this room.

Grand acted upset over the little ones' hanging back. But he turned our way, grinning anyhow. "You're scared is all. And you're damned smart to be. Still, I guess you can see her okay from out there. Here's your grandmother. She's why you're here."

I watched him try to help the woman. He lifted a glass and water pitcher; he poured some, spilling. She was beyond drinking from a glass; he tipped wet against her lips anyhow, it ran all down her chin, darkening her nightie. He did this with the heavy-handed earnestness his stories showed.

Grand touched her forehead, pressed the hair back. "You kids want to leave, probably. And who can blame you, seeing her like this?" The corners of his mouth went up as for a smile, but it wasn't one. His hand tested her for fever. Grand acted possessive even of Ruth's dying.

He just shook his head. "You children don't like it now, but you've seen enough so you'll pretty much remember. Yeah, this woman here, this old woman here . . ."

And he picked up a hairbrush from the bedside table; he made a few swipes at her yard-long hair. The man grinned like a salesman demonstrating. "Ever seen such hair?

Maybe he hoped to show us this was beautiful, that she was still beautiful. But to me, it was not. She was not.

I can't bear recalling this next part but—as Grand predicted—I do . . . do remember. Some white hair lifted by his brush got tangled in the clear tubes leading to her nose. Then I reached for some support not there, I had to lean against the doorjamb. My cousins noticed. Since I was the oldest, dutiful and all . . . I didn't—but I'd come so close to fainting. It was the smell of her room, the scorched steam heat; it was seeing how long a person's hair had always secretly been, it was all the sweetish flowers everywhere. I told myself, "Grownups use flowers to mean this, *too.*"

At a red light two blocks from the hospital, he reminded us—already bickering in back, glad to again be loud spoiled Grafton brats, "Your grandmother came from money. Not like my people. Money always made her so particular. She scolded me something fierce, remember? Yeah, I could always count on Ruth for that. Merciless, she was. Merciless, hard, lovely woman. You had to admire her. I never stopped admiring her to pieces. She always *kept* herself so nice . . . Ruth." Then we watched Grand fall across the steering wheel.

At first I thought, He is having an attack. You are the oldest. Run. A hospital's just blocks away. Go fast. They'll help. "Attack"—that was all I knew about old people dying: attacks so often got them. Hers'd happened in the garden, then she crawled, on all fours, up toward the porch; but her attack, it found her there, too.

Us kids slowly figured: Grand was only weeping. We probably felt more embarrassed about the man's sobbing than if he'd perished at the wheel. "He's *cry*ing," our fussy youngest said. "He's crying like *you* would, Sandy." "Would not." "Would so." But nervousness soon hushed them.

He made sounds like a child doing poor animal imitations. The traffic light changed three times. It being un-rush hour in downtown Falls, North Carolina, in 1964, only three cars had gathered behind us. The first tried pulling around without even honking (it was that long ago), but the car needed more room. So finally the driver hit her horn once, wincing, lifting her shoulders.

My youngest, sulkiest girl cousin—who'd said "No" and "Yisch" at the hospital—now sulked. "We're *block*ing things. We're messing *up* everything. I hate this part." Though her sassiness shamed me, I understood—its bossy tone (inherited?) might just reach him now. "Well." Grand struggled to sit, wiping his eyes on the roof of either hand. "Mustn't do that. Don't want anybody complaining about their Little Bobby." Us kids looked at each other. Four child hands touched his shoulder, touched the lined, glazed neck. Our Packard lurched forward just as the light turned red. A screeching bread truck swerved to miss us. Sidewalk shoppers covered their upper faces. "Joyride," Grand explained to the dashboard. His eyes were locked straight ahead. We all sat in back. We kept very still, not exactly holding hands (it was not that kind of family) but feeling comforted by all the cousinly little legs and shoulders pressing against our legs, our shoulders.

With her gone—everybody saw how much she'd really done for him. Meaning: everything. It was just unbelievable. Things you couldn't even name—except by saying, "Something's off, *some*thing's wrong. Did he have two shoes on today?—probably, but something . . . else." His driving grew wilder. It got so when locals saw his Packard Skipper in motion, their cars pulled right to the roadside, as if honoring a funeral. People new to town complained, not having the full history. Our sheriff's parents had once enjoyed six months' free rent in 1931 in a toolshed behind my grandfather's garage. Sheriff Wilks refused to give Grand so much as a warning. "Mustn't embarrass Mr. Grafton," our one-man police force said to strangers. "Mr. Grafton has a lot *on* him just now." Folks new here snapped back, "Your Mr. Grafton is a menace to society and I dearly hope it's your squad car he totals."

The dark Packard now seemed everywhere, in sudden need of washing. It quickly filled with litter—proof that Grand ate, against his daughters-in-law's wishes, fast food out on the Strip by our mall. "You mustn't let him go *near* that highway," Mother scolded my father. "Once he's on 301, it'll probably mean instant death for him and many others."

"But how can *I* stop him? A court injunction, what?" Dad asked us all. "He's my father. How can I stop him?" We heard: Dad really wanted advice, even from us kids. We all sat quiet at dinner, thinking of the world's hazards, traps set everywhere for babies, animals, old people.

You started wondering, Had *she* washed the Packard all those years—a woman so intent on not knowing how to drive? "You think Mother went out there at 2 A.M. with a hose and sponge? Maybe she wore some of his flashier old clothes. Can't you just picture her?" Dad smiled. I could. (I'd felt so shamed by Grand's weeping in the car, I never told my folks.) To me at twelve, his relying so on Ruth seemed unmanly, disappointing. Scary how a man can need one woman. Ruth had warned us all those years. We thought it was just another part of their cross-with-each-other routine.

For the first time in memory, my own mother began to speak fondly of my bossy, edgy, late grandmother.

Father hired a cleaning woman to live in and cook for Grand. Three quit in one month. Two ladies claimed he followed them around all day, they felt observed. Even while they vacuumed as loudly as possible, Grand shouted gory Falls sagas their way. Bank robbers, understandable hangings, infant lockjaw. One woman complained, "The old gentleman keeps hounding me with stories about the dead, and they don't *go* anywhere, they're just *end*less. Besides, he made certain . . . I think they were . . . advances." By now I was being sent away to school. I remember marveling that anybody would quit to avoid Grand's tales. But then, of course, I was safely someplace else. I was a year past thirteen; I now resisted Sunday visits to Grand's. If forced to go, I stayed on the porch with my opinionated aunts and suddenly-not-bad-looking girl cousins. He shuffled out and gave me wounded, amused looks—made more unbearable by their basset-hound forgiveness. Now older, safe at school, I could afford to be sentimental about the man's repeated "good ones." I felt myself to be more sophisticated than he and so decided Grand was, like the folk music then in vogue, "colorful."

My Northern roommate grilled me, Wasn't Little Bobby really just your basic "slum lord"? Didn't he lease to the white merchants who overcharged blacks?

At school, around 2 A.M., stoned illegally, I tried ignoring this, tried telling my suitemates one about Lancaster's mule. Before I even got near the punch line, my pals walked out. "Guess . . . you had to've *been* there," I explained to an empty dorm room. Maybe turns-of-speech involving mules just didn't cut the mustard after 1962, didn't translate beyond Falls's city limits. Maybe Little Bobby Grafton would always remain an acquired taste. *I* now considered him remarkable—but my own reasons might be genetically determined, too simple to quite name or recognize. Maybe Grand's charms could never be explained by a college-bound "Bryan"? Only some Willy could tell the plain and salty truth of "Ears" Grafton, loving witness to others' wit, the not-pretty poor kid who lived in trouble, who met and wooed a dowried lady worthy of satin sheets. A sharecroppers' kid who, though often crossed, never ever snitched, not once.

For the month after her funeral, he refused to leave their

house. He seemed afraid Ruth might return and not find him waiting. Then we heard how Mr. Grafton had paid unannounced social calls on two recent widows. These handsome women were confused when he sat beside them on settees, saying little while glaring hard at their wrists, their necks. Maybe Bobby planned to appear amorous. He first looked peeved, then dangerous. He slid onto one knee, tried kissing a lady's hand the way some foreign baron might. She yelped, set her pug dogs barking, showed him out. Hoping to lighten things, Grand smiled. "I guess *you* know why everybody says 'tighter'n Lessie Poland's boot', huh?"

"Why you say *what*?" (She was new here.)

When he turned up at my folks' place, Grand wasn't wearing mourning black. He arrived in plaids-over-stripes. Knotted around his neck, one unclean polka-dotted bow tie. Most of a piece of blueberry pie was crusted on it, the archaeology of a good meal. My mother first tried teasing him, hoping the indirect approach might work. "What?" He stared at his own ragamuffin outfit. "Myself, I can't see it, Helen. To me it's all just clothes. Lucky to have them. They cover you, they come in different colors, so what?"

Mother said she really should take his bow tie off and go out in our back yard and bury it like a dog would bury a bone. Then, hearing herself, Mother laughed, adding, "I'm beginning to sound like . . ." but she hushed, quit smiling. He looked up then. "Like who? *Say* her name. I want to hear you say her *name*, Helen."

"Like Ruth," Mother said. "I was going to say I sounded like Ruth complaining she was sounding too much like you."

He grinned, nodding—jaunty. "She was merciless, okay," and tears—sudden amazing amounts—came pouring down a face the color of boiled ham.

This business about the mixed-up clothes might sound like nothing, really. But you'd be surprised how strange and funny it can look, how disturbing. With Ruth alive, Bobby usually wore white shirts, dark trousers, black business shoes, and semi-loud ties (his wife's one concession to the taste of a man who admired carny-barker types like Buck Lancaster). Grand loved having youngbloods around town call, "Mighty flashy hand-painted tie you got you there, Mr. Grafton." "*I* thought so." He'd wink.

But now at the mall, Grand appeared a sad hick farmer arrived to purchase some item expensive as a tractor—some guy fearful of being taken, maybe thinking he'd blend in better if hidden by the right number of city plaids.

When I came home from school, my folks drove Grand and all of us to a new restaurant. The organist was playing, the place was dark, Grand was offered a large black leatherette menu. Finally he leaned across the table, whispered to me, "Where are the *numbers* of the hymns listed, Will? She always marks my hymns for me."

Others heard. My father offered the benefit of the doubt. "Like church, Daddy? 'Good one.' " The old man's face changed; he grabbed my father's wrist, hard. Grand then checked around and—world's worst liar—forced a grin. "Don't *I* know? Didn't I plan that? My own flesh and blood, and it can't even take a joke?"

We laughed. Yes. Oh, *ha* ha ha.

My father was at his law office meeting with six bigwig clients come to file a class action; Grand popped in unannounced. The secretary had just adjourned to the bathroom, Grand passed her desk and shuffled through double doors into the conference room. Little Bobby hadn't shaved for a week. He wore red bedroom slippers, a tasteful windbreaker, and a striped shirt, but he'd put the windbreaker on first. He carried, for some reason, a can of 3-in-1 oil. "How a*bout* this weather?" He settled at the long, teak table. When people stared, he smiled. "Hot enough for you?" Soon as my dad got the conference uneasily restarted, Grand nodded off, sitting upright,

snoring tenderly. Since the six clients were not from Falls, it
all proved harder to explain. These were the kind of high-
powered folks who might've called a sheriff if they saw some
vintage Packard weaving lane to lane. New people.

Such business-hour visits happened often after that. My
father was too shy or kind to tell Grand his turning up unin-
vited was not exactly . . . convenient. When the old man barged
in on meetings with locals, Dad could say, "You've all met my
father." But with important out-of-towners, Dad shrugged, "A
relative," adding, quieter, "Period of grieving here." Dad confessed at dinner, "Listen, you all, it might get worse. I'm one
step away from 'I've never seen this man before in my life.' "
We laughed. What else could you do? Grand had stayed too
lucid for locking up in some home. But, interrupting another
legal meeting, Bobby told one Yankee client, "Yeah, brought
Arthur downtown with me today." "Really?" The woman
looked around for help; Father sat rubbing the bridge of his
nose. "Yeah." Grand winked. "Arthur-*it*is."

"Ah-ha."

Sheriff Wilks, a man of principle, refused to revoke
Grand's license, even when Mother drove down with some
brownies, then begged. Two days in a row Grand was found
patrolling our county courthouse. He had come, he told some
carpenters working on office partitions, to buy the title for a
twenty-acre farm five miles southeast of town, the old Redmond place, please. Grand knew the soil there very well. He
had decided it'd be perfect for soybeans and now wanted to
buy it as a little family spread. He needed it at once. He had
the money on him. He was walking around showing strangers
this great wad of hundred-dollar bills.

The county registrar—a family friend—noticed him and
was very patient and helped him look up the deed. She phoned
my parents only on finding that Redmond had died in 1880
and that Grand's own father had bought the tract at auction,
had fallen behind with payments, and, in 1912, lost it. These

twenty acres were zoned for business around 1946. The old mall had stood right there since late '62.

I was home from school. I planned mailing a turquoise bracelet and some philosophy paperbacks to my girlfriend—stuck at home on vacation with *her* parents. At the Falls post office I spied one old-timer flipping through Wanted posters. He wore green fishing boots, coveralls, a seersucker suitcoat. The same Wanted signs have hung on the wall since I was a kid. Other people noted the old guy; they slowed for a second, then maneuvered gingerly around him. People seemed to consider him harmless—but also about as crazy as . . . as an I don't know what.

I have to say this on my behalf. I was sixteen, a delicate age for enduring public scenes and family embarrassments. I headed toward my grandfather. He would be glad to see me. I could make a joke: "Found any good bank robbers lately?" "Got Arthur along?" something. Then I noticed that, at a table marked with today's date, he was using the chained ballpoint. He'd got some paper towels from the bathroom (when I was sixteen, clean restrooms were still open to the public in all U.S. post offices!). The towels appeared covered with finely printed notes. He must've lingered here all morning, transcribing. A Styrofoam cup of cold-looking coffee waited on one marble ledge. He slumped forward, jotting, muttering, secretive. I still felt I could handle this. I took a few steps closer, when I saw the drawings. He was copying one criminal's face. He was trying to.

He'd done other portraits. Some of these sketches were weirdly good, carefully shaded with blue ballpoint. His being able to actually sort of draw—that made it all seem worse to me and weirder. Since early morning, he'd been down here for every citizen of Falls to see. Was he trying to memorize likely fugitives? Did he want to recollect certain faces he'd known and lost, like the mug of shady, witty Lancaster? Would Grand now drive along the streets of Falls, bounty-hunting crooks?

I never knew. I stared at the back of this man, his farmer's neck so deeply creased it pleated. Others stayed clear of him. One passing older woman saw me noticing. She offered the brisk eye-rolling look that sane nervous strangers give each other. It's ugly. It means: "Sad, yes. But *we're* not like him."

What I did next—I told myself—was really out of pity, gratitude, even love. After all, he seemed so happy, so busy over there.

I slipped out the side exit.

Four days before Grand died, Mother played hostess to a regional Master's Bridge Championship. I personally consider card games fairly silly, waste of everybody's time. But back then bridge was important to her.

Over the years, five people have made it their mission to teach me the game. We endure one nice long comical evening; then they each mercifully give up on me. I beg them to. Even so, I'd played enough to know the game and—over one bored rainy Christmas vacation spent in Falls recovering from pneumonia—I saw what a genius my mother was at it. She has a mind that any captain of industry might covet. I don't know who to blame for her wasting it on cards. Society? or her? or cards themselves? Odd, *she's* never really seemed all that miffed about the waste. So what are you going to do?

The championship at our house mattered not at all to me, but I'd seen her planning it for months. And so, though I was sixteen and though this proved hard, I stayed out of her way and, for once, kept my irony to myself.

The limo of our governor's wife was double-parked out front. A uniformed driver buffed its chrome—a cake-decoration-sized state flag rode each fender and looked fairly absurd there. I was a kid. So much of the world then looked ridiculous to me—but these flags, I think, still would.

Our house held ninety distinguished white women. Card tables were arranged everywhere, ashtrays and chairs borrowed from the caterer. I'd retreated to my room upstairs but could hear a musical chatter-natter. It already sounded like a great chummy success.

I remember the next part in this order: I came sneaking down the backstairs, eager for a secret lunch snitched off can-apé trays. I knew from other parties how ninety visiting ladies just love catching sight of the household's big-eared if not-un-handsome teenaged son. They really check you out, shame-less, giving you the once-over from the feet up. I hated that. I hated acting polite to grownups I didn't respect. I didn't respect many adults then. I did not yet understand what they had to put up with.

So I'm dodging down our backstairs when I hear two State Bureau of Investigation detectives drag in a whimpering man. They had him by his wrists. He thrashed between them in the foyer, pleading loud, "You're *hurt*ing Arthur." His pants were covered with sticky seedpods from some walk through some woods. He wore a shirt with buggy races occurring all across it. His fly was unbuttoned and a goodly number of the printed racing buggies tufted out there as at some finish line. He wore a rolled knitted sailor's cap from the Army-Navy outlet; he sported a green clip-on bow tie. There was about him the look and scent of a fellow too smart, absentminded, or aggrieved to bathe very often.

Two young men wrestled him from the living room, where our governor's wife had just ceased dealing. They pushed him more towards Mother. She rose, gone ash-white, frowning as at some difficult eye chart. "Smarts," the old man stated. "These boys are big and they keep *hurt*ing me." My mother and I hollered it at the same moment, *"Let him go!"*

Since she hadn't seen me on the stairs, my voice made her jump. She spun this way, gave a long, freighted look up the steps, a look that might be freely translated *"Oh, shit.* Darling, what are we to *do* here?"

"Ma'am, we caught him hiding under your neighbor's car-port. When he spotted us watching, he got down on all fours behind a hedge, then made a break for your house. Calls himself Arthur. Claims to know you, ma'am."

My mother nodded. "He did . . . does." She was fairly panting now. Her fixed, grieving smile just slayed me. I eased down the stairs, hoping to be of use—still her dutiful eldest.

In silence, Mother's face told me, "Darling, if you get him out of here right now before it's even worse, I'll give you anything in the world, *any*thing."

But as I stepped toward my grandfather, now released and massaging his thin reddened wrists, he noticed ninety women. Some gazed down from the stair landing. They'd gone dead quiet on the sunporch. Grand toured a crowded, frozen dining room; he stalked the living room—progressing rubber to rubber. The old man frowned at a house suddenly paved with card tables, four well-appointed women settled at each, all holding cards like geisha hand fans in the air before them. The women were quite correct to gape back at him. His arriving between two state agents was reason enough, but the clothes drew a little extra attention.

Then Grand smiled over at Mother. He'd got it. His sun-cooked face spread—wonderful with pleasure. "Helen, why, you sly dog you! You've gone and opened a rest-aurant. That's a good one. Always did claim you were smart, I don't care what Ruth said. Now every inch of your place is a little moneymaker, right? You little thief. And still pretty as a speckled puppy, too. Just look at all the suckers you've stuffed in here. Hi, ladies! Why, it's right cozy. You kept it *like* a house, but you're not leaving your customers too much extra legroom—packing them in like sardines, eh, you operator? You got it all over that son of mine. He still having a hard time making a go of the office? I hope you two don't *need* a restaurant. But, sugar, tell Little Bobby something off-the-record-like—how'd you get around the *zon*ing?"

And he winked.

Mother was far too stunned to hush him as he wandered. It was too late. There could be no future. He free-associated aloud, pausing to half-stoop—admiring whatever showed of nyloned legs on certain younger bridge enthusiasts.

I cannot describe to you the silence in our house just then.

Mother, using eyebrows only, swinging her head, hinted: I should maybe take him to the back yard, maybe? Very quickly, maybe? But first she did something I will always love her for.

By now he was entertaining ladies in the living room, gabbing about his constant companion Arthur. Mother walked up behind Grand. When his face turned toward hers, Mother's—oval, cordial—went instantly serene. The farmer grinned back, entranced with her beauty and business sense. These two people stood for one second, face to face. Watching, I forgot everything unpleasant. (There's a moment when every itchy sixteen-year-old boy suddenly *sees* his mother, sees her whole—and when he knows for the first time, "Hey, my mother is 'a brunette,'" when he understands that she's a not-at-all-unattractive woman of thirty-five and is desirable and good, and when he really really wants to run away with her forever. This, for me, was that moment.) What she did: she put one palm on Grand's shoulder and—while he smiled back at her simply, so simply—her free hand touched his stubbled cheek. Then Mother said loud enough for everyone downstairs to hear, "Ladies, I want you to meet my father-in-law. A dear man."

Then I led him out.

The party chugged on, but its tones now sounded clogged; it would end early. I've always hated her guests for leaving so soon. I mean, doesn't everybody have a family? Shouldn't they have understood? And my mother never got over it, either. This sounds trivial, I know, but the things that really shave the years off everybody's lives are often just this slight. —No fair.

I kept my hand on the small of Grand's back and, exiting through the kitchen, grabbed a fistful of trimmed sandwiches for us. I squired him to a group of lawn chairs in the sun; I settled at the foot of his chaise. He had gobbled four sandwiches before really noticing me. Then half-standing, reaching into his pants' pockets—he pulled out the little can of household oil, one uncut plug of Sweet Peach chewing tobacco, and a ruby-chip dinner ring now missing four stones.

"How do *you* like my bow tie?"

I smiled. "What, are you taking a poll?"

"It's just . . . nobody seems to . . ." and Grand held on to both ends of it the way a clown would. I felt he was putting me on, he'd been tricking all of us, hoping to unload faulty goods at top dollar, at night. For a second, it seemed Bobby'd finally become the kind of flimflam artist he'd always admired. But the moment passed. I saw he hadn't pulled a thing; there was no "good one." Instead, here in direct sun—a forelock of white hair, ears seriously testing the rolled cap—was one very old and cruelly healthy senile man. He'd once been so charming. He could no longer regulate it.

"Yes, sir. Quite a tie. 'Seriously groovy,' some people'd say." (It was 1968, not that it matters.) He shifted toward our house, frowning, maybe guessing he'd just made a mistake. Toilets flushed upstairs and down—ladies discussing recent events clear of their hostess's hearing. I thought: Poor Mother. Then decided: But poor Grand here, too. Poor all of us eventually and now.

Touching the items spread before him, he shifted these, a shell game. Grand stared at me, as if trying to recall something. Yesterday I'd avoided him at the post office; I blamed that for today's embarrassments. He pointed my way, saying to nobody, "Look, a boy. What is he, about eighteen?"

"I'm almost seventeen. *I* am. I'm *here*. Say it to *me*. It's Willy, Grand."

"You seem older. Than that. And know what, buddy? You definitely *look* like somebody. Seems like I should *know* you."

Breath failed me for a second. (A civic thought: And they're letting him drive around in a car like this?)

Slowly I explained who I was, via my connection to him. I skipped being Bryan, I stuck with Willy.

"That a fact? Well, you know, one look at you and I someway *said* to myself, I said . . . I went . . . went . . ."

" 'Little Bobby' . . . ?' "

"Little Bobby! The very name. You're smart, aren't you? Not as smart as . . . Little Bobby, but smart."

I noticed secret-service men watching us from around the house. I felt furious—I considered flipping them the finger, then remembered dodging this very gentleman downtown.

So I decided to tell him a story. It was all I could think of. Keep him occupied. If he trotted back into the house, we'd all have to move from Falls. I started with one of his that you know, one about a local livestock dealer.

Afterward, he sat rearranging the can, tobacco, and ring—like hoping to sell them. Soon as I finished "Lancaster's Mule," Grand nodded. "You must've told me that one before. Why's that so familiar?"

"Because it's yours. I mean it *was* yours, first. And see, you told me so if you ever forgot it or didn't care about it anymore or whatever—then *I'd* remember it and tell it back to you, see?"

"Oh," he said. "That lady is smart. She's put about thirty tables in her front rooms and the hall, even on her landing. She's soaking them good, I bet. (Why didn't I think of it at *our* house that's so empty?) Say four women eat at every table, and if she charges them, oh, maybe five bucks a head . . ."

Grand leaned nearer suddenly, voice gone stupid, manly, matter-of-fact. He said, "I bet I can beat *you* up."

I scouted for the detectives, suddenly glad they were near. I bet he *could.* I'd have a rough time hitting him back.

But Grand had already coasted past his challenge. I sat looking at him. I could. He always let you. I hated how I'd denied him in a public place. He might've hinted what he was doing there, copying convicts' photographs. Maybe he'd finally found some scam, a "good one." Now I'll never know what Grand had in mind. And I only needed to ask. He would've told me.

The next Thursday, just after dawn, seeing a Packard parked sideways at the far edge of our oldest mall's huge lot, Sheriff Wilks found Bobby Grafton in the back seat, dead. My grandfather was wearing—my parents explained later by phone—his best gray suit, one they'd forced him into for Ruth's funeral. He'd parted his hair in the very exact middle. He had on a white shirt and blue tie, and his shoes weren't bedroom slippers and were shined, and they matched.

It was just what Ruth once loved to show her Bobby off in, and now he'd picked the outfit by himself and—as planned—on a site adjoining hers—was buried in it.

The old mall is a fairly good mall as malls go. But I really wish he hadn't died there. I wish Little Bobby had made it out to some countryside he'd owned before selling cheap on the brink of its prospering. But then Dad reminded us how Grand's boyhood farm—the twenty acres that his folks could not afford for long, a truck farm with its early-blooming hollyhocks—how that rested right beneath where Big Elk Browse 'n' Buy Mall got built in '62. Grand's Packard found the spot, but not the place.

[3] SOON...

The day I learned the meaning of Lancaster's mule, I overheard a local woman use the term downtown. Odd how that happens. You wonder what *else* you've steadily missed. I had long since left home and settled elsewhere—first Cambridge, then here in New York. I now plan to hurry toward our story's end. I rush, compensating for an inherited tendency toward storytelling longwindedness. This is the part where you find out what Time did to everybody left alive. This is the part where you see how Stories maybe offer us a little dealmaking revenge on Time.

My parents and aunts unloaded Bobby's house four weeks

after his well-attended funeral. A major selling point: the fine porch on three front sides. Suddenly it'd become "the old Grafton place." It sold for under fifteen thou. North Carolina real estate always seems a bargain compared to Manhattan's, but twelve-five for such a roomy, boxy home is—even by local standards—a deal and a half.

Bobby'd let the place slide at the end, and it did look fairly bad and needed paint. But—as we grumpy grandkids pointed out—it had stayed structurally sound. Why sell, and so cheap? Ruth's good furniture was divided up. Her Aubusson carpet caused the only ugly feud. (In-laws behaved much worse than did blood relations. "I want *none* of it," my mother said.) Nobody claimed a hideous orange chair and footstool, but everybody said somebody really should. "Though, of course, where would you *put* it?"

A young couple expecting twins bought the place. He's chief DJ at Falls's Easy-Listening Rock station. This made us grandkids moan the louder: Little Bobby's heirs feel that rock should be hard, money is to enjoy, children should be seen and heard. Even a hog is wise enough to love its local life. The new owners had every right to paint our holy shrine that overly tart Williamsburgy blue—a gift-shoppe color. Driving past, I feel literally nauseous. On the front porch, near where Ruth frisked an incoming Grand for rent checks or criticized his outgoing outfits, one tastefully white plaster burro now stands, mopey, almost life-sized. Why a burro in Falls? It supports saddlebags sprouting geraniums that might or might not be real geraniums. I've never walked far enough into these per- fect strangers' yard to check.

For twelve-five, maybe *I* should've bought the place. But why? To do *what* with?

When Dad retired, my parents got rid of their own subur- ban house. They chose Bermuda, of all places, but soon admit- ted feeling half homesick among the hibiscus. They returned to Falls and bought a little cabin down by Indian Creek. Now they spend three months a year in our hometown, nine in

Bermuda. This pleases me very much. I visit them, but only in Falls; I never set foot on dull gorgeous Bermuda. None of my New York friends can understand this.

My spoiled girl cousins have prospered and scattered; they enjoy serious careers and have kids who're nearly done with college. Hard to believe. My spirited girl cousins all turned out fairly great-looking. They've withstood the usual serial marriages. For some reason, as a group, they're just unbelievably foul-mouthed. They remain the blond family members who look the way I think I should, but don't . . . yet. They keep their hair long, professionally full around the ear area. (Our family joke and family shame.) These cousins phone me when they're passing through New York. We meet for drinks at overpriced places, where we talk about our adored low-rent grandfather and prudish grandmother, and get positively shitfaced and cry sometimes. Round by round, our Southern accents grow humid as bad actors', till we reel onto the sidewalk, are hit in the face by Yankee winter, then holler for taxis, our tones gone suddenly harsh as any Bronx truck drivers.' Gentility will not snag you that cab during a snowstorm at 3 A.M.

(Little Bobby? Sir, your brood is finally sophisticated enough to just enjoy you to pieces. Where are you, now we're ready, "Ears"?)

I suppose that every county in our nation once enjoyed its own terms based on famous-for-around-here characters. These phrases are like most of us in being well known and useful—but within fairly strict local limits.

So, yeah, language *is* like love. Whatever phrase shows the rawest life, that finds its way into our speech. Whatever terms grow ossified and fussy, those get chipped away. If something means enough to enough people, if it really clarifies, feels accurate, then it catches on, it spreads. If our poisoned world still matters enough to enough people, then I guess they'll keep continuing. If not . . . well, not.

When I return to Falls for summer visits or Christmas, I begin to see exactly who Bobby Grafton was/wasn't. A very homely hick kid, he longed to own nice town things; and he got some, too. He let his renters slide if they talked as well as he did. His funeral was attended by 110 black people. The guy was loved. But a crusader? Moral beacon? Ha! Quite early, I'd started seeing him whole. I drove up and down one weedy street where no soul cared to live but many did. Roofs leaked, missing windowpanes sealed shut with tinfoil and Scotch tape. The landlord of all? My ex-tenant-farmer Grand—home on his porch rereading *True Detective.* At age fourteen or so, me and my girl cousins secretly mailed part of our allowance money to Dr. King's civil-rights campaign. In plain brown envelopes (at the donor's request) we got back leaflets asking "Where Are the South's White Leaders? To Whom Shall We Speak?" In Falls, I sometimes still hear the phrase Grand taught me at age ten. Experts claim the National Nightly News has homogenized regional quirks out of our national language. I'm glad that's not true quite yet. I've heard Falls citizens apply "crazy as Lancaster's mule" to myself as a part-time radical graduate student, to myself during a brief intense early partnership with a woman who wanted my heirloom ears "cosmetically pinned"; I've heard it describe my second marriage to a person "rich enough to start a foundation, old enough to be your mother." I'm comforted, knowing that a term coined mid-hog auction in 1890 still pertains.

Lately, the phrase grows more and more appropriate. Maybe, like me, you read the papers. I sometimes look up from a particularly rancid front page; I scan the air packed before my face. Say I've read about some group blowing up a plane with passengers and the terrorists themselves inside it. I shake my head the way Little Bobby would. I go, "People now . . . the world now—I swear to God, crazy as Lancaster's mule."

I know my tone might seem that of someone fairly provincial, somebody well over thirty-nine. But here in the city, many nights I feel like a perpetual outlander. To Bobby, this city—its onyx towers, crystal towers—might look alien as Mars. My apartment is on the fortieth floor. I sit watching skyscraper lights come on. I sometimes feel very old here. Especially at the end of an office day, with tonight's news smudging my hands.

I'm not the first to notice: it's dangerous, what's happening. I mean, something's wrong, so *off.* We must all be very very careful.

What can a person do? Well, you stuff the offending newspaper into the trash, you go get a night's sleep and, come morning, decide to make an excellent omelette. You do what you can. (An omelette for one. Between marriages, childless, I sometimes wish I'd got custody of something, somebody. In this, I am like many of my friends: I seem to manage the career thing pretty much okay. But I've never ever really got the hang of the love part. Not yet, anyway.)

During breakfast I can't help noticing—this milk carton is coated with Wanted posters. Posters no longer seek the hurters. The hurt ones are now shown. Missing kids. Lost to what? To maniacs, or black holes, or a new child-slave trade? Where've they all *gone*?

People do get used to this, right? Tell me people get used to this.

I think about Falls in 1962. I know I'm being an escapist. So what? Thanks to Little Bobby, I remember a hometown of ladies' bustles, genius crooks, gold watches big as three-egg omelettes. Falls 1962 might've been Falls 18 and 62. I picture mules, not Packards. Hey, whatever *happened* to his Packard? Boy, would I love to have that Packard now.

In present-day New York, my first name is mostly only "Bryan." Sometimes, with certain young-women-strangers, I do try changing. "You know," one told me recently, "even from across this bar, you somehow looked like a Willy." "I thank you, ma'am," said Bryan.

Oh, to resurrect Little Bobby Grafton. Even for one night. You and "Ears" and me could really step out then. Willy here would surely throw around the plastic. Maybe it's a sign of our times, my wanting to spend big on our honored guest. We'll wine and dine him all over high-tech Manhattan, squiring Grand everywhere—to hear café singers, to see punk clubs downtown. Once back from rabble-rousing, I'll keep him awake for the 6 A.M. news. Imagine what he'll say about this place, this moment.

Home, I'll settle Little Bobby near my choicest window in my favorite chair. It's upholstered in pigskin. I won't turn on any lamps; the city's commercial glare is trapped (an oxblood color) under low clouds. In here, there's light enough to read by. I imagine Grand staring out at the skyscrapers opposite; I imagine him wondering aloud if the renters on top pay less than those more grounded. Bobby asks where city people wash their cars. He wants to know if, all along, I *planned* to live alone like this. My answer: "Well, sir—yes and no."

Tired, he'll hunker deep into my Scandinavian easy chair, his ankle-high black shoes propped on the matching footstool. I'll go and warm a little low-fat milk for him. From the kitchen, I can ask things. I mostly see his chair back, one hand curled on the armrest. I want to hear Grand say: Oh, it's really not so bad—the world now—and it's not too late. Maybe things just need to go back some, get fortified—a bit more local. Meaning what? I doubt that Grand will say this. But look, I can hope, can't I?

What realm did those moral tales prepare us for? Once, I had a childish silvery idea: the Future.

I stand stirring the saucepan, trying to keep his milk from scorching. I see Bobby by the window, a dark silhouette against the crossword puzzle of bright windows, neon names of Japanese computer firms. He appears so small and wizened in a high-backed glove-leather chaise. (For some reason, it costs me two thousand dollars, plus tax.) Grand manages to tilt the whole thing back a notch, he praises the apartment buildings opposite. They're tall enough to wear red lights, warning away low planes. He calls how I sure do have boo coo neighbors, don't I? Are they mostly nice? He's already loosening his tie, fumbling through pockets, getting ready for bed.

His chair's beside a formica cube—one sold not as "table" but as "freestanding modular unit." Onto this, Bobby empties each linty pocket. I see the busy knotted hand; callouses have quilted it into a catcher's mitt. Out he fishes the gold watch, its chain dangles little brass horseshoes once considered lucky. Stub fingers wind the watch, and with some delicacy—a fringe of white hair tips into view; one substantial ear presses against gold casing. His head half nods—the watch is put off to one side. Pocket change gets piled into neat columns by denominations. A small pocketknife emerges, shy in the city (but no self-respecting county man would leave home without one).

The stained driver's license, then half a pound of landlordly keys: access to rental homes, livestock barns, red Allis-Chalmers tractors.

Finally, on top, thumb and forefinger place the keepsake ring, some rubies left (if just in chips). Done, the hand slides back toward its counterpart; they join over the lap, and before I can pour Grand's milk into my best mug, slow snoring unfolds. I shake my head and grin some, muttering. I step into the room, I lean against one wall, studying the back of his chair, my chair. So much to ask and him asleep. *Is the world blind or does it just not give a damn?*

Between my own smooth hands, this hot cup feels so good. Automatically both eyes close. I hold on for dear life—I live here now.

Stuck in the present on the fortieth story, Willy is still interested, but waiting. I keep listening, I stay primed for something extra.

Yeah, it's me here—me, all ears. **Q**

The Donkey's Smile

The name Ita, which has for its nickname the name Itty—which was the name of my father's mistress—is the Latin word for *thus*.

Not that *ita* is a name without a certain allure—I wouldn't blame anyone if he or she felt that way, having, as *ita* does, that certain "Come here!" or that "Let's go!" to it, such as, in the Romance languages, *vas-y* does, or *avanti*, these translations being probably more familiar—the post-Christ languages, as I refer to them—than the Classics are.

Please forgive me—before I proceed any further, all these allusions, and also, I am afraid, the disjointed way in which I must go forward, being so well suited, as indeed I am, to that method of discourse with which I am familiar—that stepping ahead that a translator does quite unexpectedly to a word shimmering somewhere up there, that back-stepping, equally unexpectedly, to take back a word and put another in its place. I apologize in advance should anyone carried along by this find him or herself, due to a fault in the logic of this, tripped somewhere between the paragraphs—or plunged, to be a bit more graphic. Which is why, in case you have been wondering, when so many of my colleagues have forsaken it for that most enduring of bonds, or so it is intended, I have chosen, rather, to cherish and sustain it—that faculty I have of going backward and forward—*cum placeat*, I believe the phrase to be—whenever it pleases me.

Speaking, however, of the abyss that by taking a step here or a step there one might always fall into, I have found myself all this while not attending to the direction in which I have been leading you but preoccupied as we go along with a little joke—although *joke* seeming a little too labored for what happens with as little resistance as what happens in what I am about to tell you—which was told to me, incidentally, by a nun—perhaps I should use the word *digression,* or the word *epigram,* or *epitaph,* etc., etc.

Well, *"Avanti,"* then, as one might say in the vernacular. There was a person, a nun, in fact, who was given a donkey to ride out and see the landscape on, the instructions for riding the donkey being that when you wanted the donkey to go forward, you had to say, "Thank you, God," and when you wanted the donkey to stop, you had to say, as if the donkey were a prayer you were putting an end to, "Amen." (And by the way, when you get to what happens—which, being as intelligent a person as you are, I do not but doubt you have seen ahead to—you will see the contrariness of my having chosen a word like *digression,* this tale having very little to do with the Latin verb *digredi*—"to go away from.")

At any rate, when the person riding the donkey, the nun, had been riding for a certain distance and been significantly distracted by that landscape—although how anyone could be distracted by a landscape as apparently flat and beauty-less as the one I have been speaking of, I cannot help remarking—although I, of all people, should well know how taste in matters similar to these, especially in the matter, say, of flatness, or of its opposite, is subject, between one person and another, to some considerable variation.

But *distracted* nonetheless is the word I will use, since what happens in my little epigram of a tale—although *epitaph* would be more telling, you will see—is that at the unforeseen moment of arriving, in such a landscape, at a ledge so steep that a person could have jumped from it and surely been killed, is that the person riding the donkey, the nun—she being the one that for now, at least, I am speaking of—having been too distracted to remember what word it was she needed to say to arrest the forward motion of the donkey, put her hands to the heavens in prayer and spoke the only word of that prayer that she had time for—the word *amen.*

At which point, of course, the donkey stopped.

Immediately after which, and now I am certain you have seen down to the end of this tale, the nun looked up again to the heavens as gratefully as any good nun would have and breathed the words—you could hardly say she spoke them, her tongue so nearly dead in her mouth—"Thank you, God."

Now, because you are smart enough, your having passed right by the first allusion of this story, the allusion to Ita, as gracefully as you did, and having seen, as I am sure you did, the plunge of that little joke before it happened, and having also seen that I am not the kind of person to embrace the embrace of as many sets of arms—when one alone would have done, or more than done—as the religion I am speaking of embraces you with, you therefore must be wondering why it is that I have such a lovely medal as the one I have, a gold medal dangling from a necklace of gleaming pearlish beads—a St. Christopher, I think it is—a fact which—my letting it dangle there—you must accept on faith, you being no more able to see it doing that, dangling there slack as the reins on a donkey that is going where it is supposed to, than you could have seen, from my physical attributes, that I had no other reason for not marrying than the one I gave you.

Furthermore, this medal having been given to me by my mother, at least I am fairly sure it was, I being plenty old enough then to remember, which I will get to in a moment, you might well ask why it is I would choose, I not being forced to do anything, I can assure you, to harness myself in something representing, as it were, my own mother's misapprehension of what my nature is, her thinking, that is, that that St. Christopher, with his strong arms carrying a child across somewhere—I suppose the child was supposed to be me—would have comforted me, or even that I would have let it, knowing by then, as finally, by the time I received it, I did, who it was, the St. Christopher she had handed me over to—albeit with a kiss; not to mention the fact that I was at this point hardly a child, hardly at the age, that is, when I could have been so easily picked up, or touched, or led across anywhere.

You see, the reason I have been putting off giving you the proof of how old I was then—which has to do with what I was doing when my mother and the woman, the one I first set off describing, were buying that St. Christopher—is that it is one of those unsavory little personal details (what I was doing when I was waiting for them), those apparently insignificant little hairs—the proof is—that are left somewhere, an insignificance, I can assure you, with which I did not wish to belittle what image I have of my mother, and would not still belittle her thus, had it not to do with this issue, the issue of age, not so much issuing forth, in the biblical sense, from that other issue, as you will see when we get there.

Because what I was doing while I was waiting (that I was old enough to have waited there alone being enough proof of what my age was, I should have thought) was pretending to be reading a book I had to read, a book, if I remember correctly, on Alexander the Great, the book opened on my knee to that part in the narrative explaining how Alexander tames a wild stallion—Bucephalus, I think his name was—by a method into which I will not go in detail, you being able to find it in Plutarch for yourself—and you should—except to say that Alexander did it by reining him in bit by bit instead of all at once, keeping the stallion turned all the while into the sun, so that the dancing and thrashing of his shadow before him might not frighten him, Alexander being then, I might add, of no more of an age to have had any more hairs on him, of the kind of which I am speaking, than at the time I had.

At any rate, with that book balancing there precariously on my knee so that at any moment I might go back to reading it if I had to, what I actually was doing was trying to twist my head around in such a position as to see under my arm—with no more success, I might add, speaking of animals, than, attempting the same maneuver, a mule would have had (and it is here, with the rendering up of the little hair, so to speak, that I ask you to try to bear with it, any squeamishness that the personal nature of this anecdote might give rise to), until

finally I had gotten what I thought I had seen there in the
morning and laid it in the margin of the book where the book
creases in—a very short, almost invisibly thin line it made
there, but a line nonetheless, which, upon closer examination,
seemed to have drawn out a point of flesh with it, as does a
honeysuckle pistil a point of honey, when suddenly out they
came too, the two of them, I shutting the book at the sight of
them—I never opened it again—devoting myself then to trying to make myself look as if, having finished the section I was
meant to have read, there remained nothing for me to do but
sit there and watch them coming toward me and wait for them
to kiss me and show me what they had bought—the two of
them coming toward me as beautiful-looking as any figures
from the mythology of ancient Greece could be, or at least one
of them, depending on which style of beauty you prefer, their
shadows rearing up and thrashing down behind them, coming
together and separating again like the shadows behind two
horses; nor could you have foretold, from one moment to the
next, which was the more powerful, an image occurring to me
for no other reason, I can assure you, than because of my
reading.

It was a shock, therefore, a reining in all at once, to make
some use of it, after all—the part about Alexander—when it
was revealed that it had been as accurate as it turned out to be,
that contest I had been describing—I am not blaming, all the
same, any outsider for thinking, as you must think too, that,
describing it as I did, I too must have known it all along, and
that, having known it all along, the first thing I should have
done was to have given to all of it the thumbs-down, the way
the emperors did, not to those persons involved in whatever
it was that I could have given the thumbs down to, I being,
although not the only one admiring those shadows, not the
one, ultimately, who chose between them—and not that my
never again opening that book—the one on Alexander—in any
way represented some childish superstition that that uproot-
ing of which I told you in such detail could in any way have

caused, or precipitated, or symbolized, even, what else was uprooted, I giving the thumbs-down, rather, to all those things that had, up to that date, been bestowed on me—that St. Christopher and the necklace it came on being not the only things I was almost lured over by, I now recall—and I apologize for having misled you if I did—that it must have been given to me, that St. Christopher, not when she leaned down to kiss me and show me what it was they had been in there deciding on—when my mother did—but sometime after.

But I hemmed and hawed, told her to take her things back, and kept them just the same, having, as I do, what in these dry countries that border the ocean they call the jawbone of the ass, by which I mean a stubborn set of temperament, there being a way in which, these things having been gotten at a certain loss, it was owed to me to keep them—the spoils of battle, as it were—those things being, since I set out mentioning them I will, so as not to have put before you false promises only, go ahead with their description (at the same time asking your forgiveness for thus digressing back to pick them up again): that St. Christopher, as I was saying, his thighs and biceps bulging; that necklace it came on, its pearls—if pearls indeed is what those beads were—having had more time to grow than I had; clothes of hers, speaking of growing, she had claimed would fit my impish shape as well as they had hers, she was younger than my mother; a bedroom chair which, having had it slipcovered quite some years ago, I have almost forgotten whom it was it came from (except when down on my hands and knees occupied in some necessity, whatever that might be, I look up to where the new fabric parts a little to reveal what it was that it came to me covered in, some sort of damask, I think it was, soft as the inside of lips, that pair of Sevres plates I use quite often, or used to use, the effect of my letting them slip from my fingers—quite by accident, I assure you—being not any more startling than had it been twelve floors up on a window ledge that it had happened from.

Of course, if you know the Old Testament (and please

excuse this falling back on it again, the topic of the jawbone), you will know how many Philistines Samson killed with it—which, in a dream, I held once too, that jawbone. A dream where across the river I saw her among the women, all of them bathing in the stream, philistines if ever there were any—the word *philistine* having come to refer to—and please excuse my feeling, unnecessary as it may be, that I have to define it—all persons quite beneath one in terms of culture or aesthetics, or any manner of intelligence—and touching each other, they all were, and when I looked more closely I could see her beckoning me all the while to come over—*"Vas-y, vas-y,"* I think it was she was saying to me, or some such other phrase—and me on the other side of that river ready to use it if I had to, the jawbone of which I was speaking, its length being, in case you have never seen one, a length that people such as yourselves, and those others of my colleagues of whom I had been speaking earlier, know well enough, but with a turn upward where it hinges to the body, which is where Samson gripped it, or at least I did in my dream, that comparison being quite amusing if you could see me, hardly a Samson, to say the least—and it having teeth all along it, teeth that could make anyone envision the living donkey curling its lips back to show them, the teeth—the donkey's smile, I call it—and the dark areas on the inside side of the teeth, the side where the tongue does its business, rubbing in and out the way any tongue does, deciding what to do.

Well, sometimes she wanted to hold my hand, Ita did, and sometimes she wanted a postcard, which, until my mother had made herself as unavailable as she had chosen to make herself, we would send Ita, and other times all Ita wanted was for me to let her give me the things the way I used to let her give them to me—which, had my mother seen ahead to, she should have stopped me from, it being no easier to overlook, in my opinion, than the edge of a cliff, and as easy to back off from as putting those words back in their rightful places—the *amen* instead of—and I am sorry to have to say it—the *thank you,* that *thank you* being, in case you have to go searching back for it, the sign to continue—and sometimes she wanted a kiss—although I am no Judas, I can tell you that, I letting go of each word she required afterward as if she had had to go in and finger up under my gum to get it out, as with a child or an animal you have to; and sometimes she wanted just to hear those words I knew she liked to hear, the ones that gave her that look of an ocean in her eyes, an ocean of desert, anyway.

(In my line of work, you see—which I should have told you sooner—not everything has to be so maudlin, so full of attachments, as otherwise you might find it—a kiss, for instance, can be just the lips pulling back as the approach is being made.

And then coming forward again, covering the teeth for when they have to touch, the lips do.

Yes, you can pluck a word out here or a word out there— Judas from the Garden of Gethsemane, to take the case in point, and insert it to stand for just about anyone, the one who fits it best being—when it could have been either of them, or any of them—the one who hands you over.

Which is something else I should have told you, the distance one must arrive at in this business where there is no perfect substitution, compromising, as one has to, a little here, a little there, submerging, as it was, almost, any other possibility, pushing that other possibility off the ledge of your consciousness—which, on its own, will happen if you let it—so that there is no looking back on it, what the old word caressed you with. Because once you have chosen, as my father liked to tell me, you have to move forward.)

Well, he was an old man by then, and she an old woman, Ita was—or older than I—when I started moving forward, I having long since passed that moment, you know the one, when the sight of your own teeth tells you what to do— not the teeth where the smile is, but the ones you set your jaw with, the ones I have been describing on the jawbone of the ass, if you will excuse the comparison, and on the inside side

that I was also describing, the side where the tongue was—
when it should have come out blessing. Starting forward, after
all that pulling and pulling and pulling against what it was I did
not want to be held by, the embrace of that St. Christopher,
so to speak, until suddenly—like something rooting itself
up—I let them let me loose a little, having somewhat thereafter let go as well, after I had succeeded at it in sufficient
measure to please at least myself, the strains of what that
profession was in which I was practiced.

Starting forward—albeit with a slight jolt—across that
landscape that was then so waterless, and still is now, as to be
growthless—except, if you consider—faint as a single hair—
the line that we were making across it—and bolting back now
and then—I was—from what the new shadow going before me
looked like, as occasionally, I must admit, still I am prone to,
and with my ears pricked up always as if to hear whatever it was
they were luring me on with—neither "Thank you" nor
"Amen," of that you need not concern yourself (although
indeed there was a time when I strained to hear those sounds),
but just his "Itty" this and his "Itty" that—which even now sets
me back another little bit when I hear it, and me correcting
him, "It's *Ita,* not Itty," "It's *Ita,* not Itty," whipping myself on,
you might almost say, he spoke her name so often.

Starting forward, she kicking and kicking and kicking, and
he up by my head urging me on more gently—the oasis already
long behind us, I could have told him—and suggesting to
her—I could hear him—that kicking and kicking was not the
way to lure anyone into going on much farther, much less a
person not quite grown—which if you saw me now, you would
not doubt at all, that I am—quite grown, I mean—not having
lost, however, as everyone who sees me notices and remarks
on, that manner of eternal youth—developmentally arrested,
as in circles more clinical than this some might call it, but
arresting nonetheless; and me mumbling, as if that string I was
leading myself along on, that was giving my steps a kind of
pacing, as I was just suggesting—that string of Ita's that is—

were the rosary of the faithless going forward, Ita being, I can't remember if I told you, the Latin word for *thus*. Until finally it was, my tongue numb with the sameness of what I was saying, and it still dangling there, as still it is—that St. Christopher on which it is written—lean down a bit closer and you will see it there—*Venite mecum et este salvi*—the translation of which, if you are interested, it being given to you by someone such as I, *Come with me and thus be safe,* you can more or less believe. *"Avanti, avanti!"* I would be crying, had I still the tongue to cry it with—until finally thus it was—our shadow now as long and quiet before us as three spires of some antique post-Christ monument, mine being the shortest—that I had carried them up out of there, out of wherever that place was where, in more ways than one, thus it had been sired—that dead-tongued child of which I have been speaking. **Q**

Figures in a Carpet

[1]

There was something different about the tapestry this
time, something in the physiognomy of the dogs, Altman
thought; something almost beyond perception, and perhaps
altogether in the realm of the imagination. A subtle change in
their attitude to the hunt, as if they were uncertain whether
they were serving the right master; a certain absence of enthusiasm for the adventure was what Altman thought he detected.

Jacob Altman had looked so often, so carefully, that he
doubted the tapestry could hold for him any additional surprises. It was one of a set of unicorn tapestries, dating from
1410–1411, that had been presented to Felix the Pious by his
in-laws, to mark his marriage to their eldest daughter. Others
in the set depicted the Commencement of the Expedition, the
young noblemen boldly setting forth with their arrows and
lances and leaping hounds; the Return, the moment when the
beautiful dead creature, its white coat stained with blood, was
presented to a pensive young maiden; and the Transfigura-
tion, the restoration of the unicorn to its former state of
health, but now safely fenced within a small garden of *milles
fleurs*. Distributed throughout the surface of each tapestry,
woven with such fine thread as to escape the notice of the
casual observer, were several sets of the respective families'
coats of arms, linked by ribbons of gold.

This particular tapestry, which according to the museum's
curators was beginning to look a bit gray and needed nothing
more than a cleaning—a laborious process in itself, the com-
plexity of which the curators could not begin to comprehend—
represented the Encounter with the Unicorn. In the midst of
a deep green forest, its floor sparkling with the petals of tiny
white lilies, the unicorn reared up on its hind legs, its great
slender horn pointing out toward the spectator. This fore-
shortening of the horn, flawed though it was, had until the

1950s caused art historians to date the tapestry from the mid-sixteenth century. With their prejudice against the so-called decorative arts, art historians had not believed that a team of anonymous tapestry weavers could, in any respect, have anticipated the spatial innovations of the great fresco makers of the fifteenth century. It was Altman's discovery of the significance of the linked coats of arms that had finally resolved the matter.

Behind and to the sides of the unicorn, hurling their lances, taking aim with their bows, blond hair flowing, nostrils flaring, thin lips curling downward in the effort, were the same young noblemen who, on the adjoining wall, had set forth so boldly. The sense of anatomy—the strain evident in the torsos beneath their loose-fitting hunting apparel, the tightening of calves within their bright red hose—was at least as advanced as that present in any painting of the period. And each face, despite its stereotyped emotion shared with each other face, bore the stamp of individuality. Once he had located the tapestry in historical time, Jacob Altman had managed to identify the various personages represented, matching their portraits to others still extant in libraries and picture collections.

But now there was the matter of the dogs, slender, short-haired, muscular dogs, white as the unicorn itself, dwarfed by its rearing bulk, nipping, in the foreground, at its hooves, drawing the attention of the unicorn away from the more lethal ministrations of their masters. In the past, Altman had not devoted much thought to the dogs. Of all the elements constituting the tapestry, the dogs seemed the least in need of explanation: just dogs, following the whims of those who kept them, honoring their canine instinct for aggression, performing their task with efficiency and zeal. Altman had occasionally in life, more frequently in dreams, encountered such dogs— just waiting for the command, waiting to be unleashed, to rip open the hide of some unwelcome, alien intruder.

But now, as he looked at the dogs, Jacob Altman felt that the zeal he had always assumed was present was simply not to be found. Its absence could not be attributed to the weavers' lack of skill: the dogs, no less than the men and vegetation, were expertly rendered, from the set of their shoulder blades to their exposed testicles. Rather, it seemed, a deliberate iconographic decision had been made to portray the dogs as unwilling agents. The animals leaped at the unicorn, it was true, but somewhat listlessly. Their gaping mouths, although exposing expanses of menacing dentition, were not actually open very wide, were not poised for action. And the look in their eyes, Jacob Altman now concluded, was unmistakable. A wide, plaintive look, sad and beseeching, tufts of eyebrow raised to express the ambivalence Jacob Altman thought some animals are so capable of. Looking into the face of their prey, two dogs spoke as follows: "We want this no more than you. Are not all of us animals? But it is better that some of us should die than all of us." And looking out at the spectator, three dogs pleaded: "We are not culpable, for we, too, are victims. We do what we must, but we do no more."

Jacob Altman at once sensed that this should be no ordinary cleaning. What was called for was a more thorough restoration, a making manifest of the heretofore somewhat covert intentions of the tapestry's creators, intentions hidden by centuries of misinterpretation.

[2]

Didn't he have enough to worry about? John Lenox flung down the Request for Intervention. The curator of Late Medieval Art wanted guidance concerning Jacob Altman, Tapestry Restorer to the World. All they had requested was a dusting—a shampoo and a vacuum—and this Altman was determined to make a federal case out of it. Couldn't they work it out without him? Serving on the Board of Trustees was proving to be a royal pain in the ass.

They liked to have a few professional people on the board, they had told Lenox; a few CEOs from major corporations, a lawyer or two, like himself. Old money was, of course, indispensable, they had said, but the real money these days was working money. People like him would ensure the long-term future of the institution. The job was strictly ceremonial, they had promised. Attend the openings, wine and dine an on-her-last-legs old lady from time to time—someone who might, with a little sweet-talking, be willing to part with that Matisse when she passed on; come in once a year to vote on the budget. That was supposed to be it.

But those curators, who were supposed to know a few things about art, they refused to straighten a picture hanging crooked without going to the board. With the constant meetings at all hours of the day, Lenox's law firm was starting to get away from him. Finally, the board had decided to handle these crises from the curatorial staff on a rotating basis, in committees of one. From now on, it would take only a single board member to approve a curator's request for permission to move a painting four feet, or to correct an attribution.

Since he'd been handling these questions alone, Lenox had assured the curator in charge of Flemish painting that it was perfectly all right to remove the glass from a painting which, the curator had been sure, would last just as long without it anyway; and he had assented to the erection of an unobtrusive barrier in front of a certain nude whose breasts seemed to attract the hands and lips of a surprising number of museum visitors; and he had allowed the date on a picture's information label to be changed from "1625–26" to "*circa* 1625."

This last was the closest Lenox had come to rejecting a request. The staffer he'd spoken with had informed him of an article that had recently appeared in a French journal. The author had suggested that the documents on which the exact dating of the painting was based—pay stubs, irritated journal entries of the artist, threatening letters from the patron, a powerful Cardinal demanding a finished product already, and then demanding a full refund—these documents were said by the article's author to be forgeries, concocted by the Cardinal's successor and intended to paint his predecessor, the patron, as an idiot when it came to the arts. Parenthetically, the staffer said, this view of the patron was still held by most art historians. A seventeenth-century squabble between a pair of priests. So, the staffer said, although the article did not make its case all that convincingly, hadn't we better play it safe and use the approximate date, 1625, since we are still sure, at least, that the work was executed around then, give or take a year or two?

"Don't you folks have any balls, any guts?" Lenox had demanded. "If it was painted in 1625 and '26—as you say— why don't you just leave it? And if you want to hedge your bets, who's stopping you? But what the hell difference could it possibly make?"

The young woman had patiently explained that more was at stake than Lenox realized. It wasn't just the one painting, she had said, it was the art history world's estimate of the acuity of the Cardinal's patronage. Had the Cardinal been a philistine who, in spite of his pedestrian taste, had made a number of important commissions, or had he been a true visionary? All of that was riding on the date on the label, because when the museum spoke on such matters, the world listened. But every time the museum spoke, the young woman added, its prestige was on the line, so should it take a chance on the scholarship of an unknown French quantity? Should the museum get in on the ground floor, at the risk of being wrong, or should it wait for the accusations and counteraccusations in the journals to pile up to the ceiling? The young woman was trembling, practically in tears, over the quandary.

"Tell you what," Lenox had suggested, conciliatorily, Solomonically, "change the date, but without the usual fanfare. No press conference, no symposium. If the Frenchy's right, we knew it all along. If he's wrong, change it back and hardly anyone's the wiser. See?" She looked as if she could have embraced him.

And now this business with the old man and his tapestry. According to the Late Medieval curator, Altman was some sort of a subversive. Lenox could deal with only one subversive at a time. At his own law firm, right under his nose, had emerged another subversive, and the whole office was in a state of uproar.

Roland was a third-year associate—B.A., Columbia; J.D., Harvard; editor of the *Law Review*. Plucked ripe from the vine, a prize catch, and best of all, he was black. Affirmative action without the gamble. All the big firms had wanted to get his name on their letterhead, and Lenox had won, and had not been let down, either. Two years plus of all anyone asked of him, burning the midnight oil all night if that's what it took; meticulous, thorough, letter-perfect, Roland was a real detail man in a profession where the details were everything.

Lenox's law firm, and all the others its size, paid well and got their money's worth. Seventy-, eighty-hour weeks for a junior associate were par for the course. But there were limits, and Lenox was always reminding his partners not to go overboard. One evening last week, three of Lenox's partners, each claiming it was an emergency, had dumped voluminous piles of papers on Roland's desk, to be analyzed and digested in a memo by the A.M. The first two stacks Roland had accepted with his customary stoicism. But the third stack was accompanied by Tilden, who, Lenox knew, was absolutely reviled by the office's younger generation. Tilden, who, master of labor relations, shortly before had circulated a memo among the associates: "I was here the other night at 10, and if I had fired a cannon down the corridor, I wouldn't have bagged a single one of you. What gives?" A loose cannon, an absolute pig, an inveterate sadist, an inventor of deadlines where there were none, Tilden was known to call people at home at four in the morning on some pretext just to hear them act polite. Plunk, down went the papers on Roland's desk and out came the gun from Roland's drawer. "Get the fuck out of here and take your fucking documents with you, you got five seconds, you son-of-a-bitch; four, three." Tilden was no fool.

Tilden, no doubt, had earned the scare, Lenox thought;

who knows, maybe he'd even learned something, although that was unlikely; but in the meanwhile, something had to be done. You couldn't run a law firm with the associates taking potshots at senior partners, it just wouldn't work. Already things were taking a turn for the worse. Lenox had heard that Roland was being hailed as a hero by some of the associates in the smaller offices, who had always been so docile. There were vague rumblings about an associates' union, collective bargaining—this, at a firm which derived substantial income from advising corporate clients on the tactics of "union avoidance," as it was euphemistically called these days.

And it wasn't going to be easy to keep this quiet. Any day now, there'd be reporters from *The American Lawyer* camped out in the lobby: "Mr. Lenox, is it true, is it true?" How many "No comments," Lenox wondered, before they turned to "informed sources"?

Lenox picked up the Request for Intervention: what Altman had in mind, the curator said, would alter, somewhat, the appearance of the tapestry, and would alter, in a somewhat more profound way perhaps, our understanding of the history of German Christianity. Altman had had radical ideas before, and so far his instincts had been on target, but the curator wanted to make sure Lenox was aware of all the pros and cons, the pluses and minuses, et cetera, et cetera. Could they meet to discuss it personally?

Oh hell! No, they could not meet personally. Let the old man have his way. At least this Altman had some balls.

[3]

The educated public knew virtually nothing of the restorer's art, it seemed to Jacob. Perhaps this was owing to the skill of its practitioners—their ability to mimic the brushstrokes of the Old Master on the easel, to imperceptibly, seamlessly meld their additions and deletions with the otherwise untouched, untouchable surfaces; or perhaps it was owing to the public's naïve faith in the power of timeless works to withstand the ravages of time, to rise above the universal tendency of materials to decay, to crack, to fade. Unbeknownst to the average, educated museumgoer, the restorer's art, in tandem with the incremental progress of science, had become a discipline of great sophistication. But in the last analysis, Jacob reflected, restoration had less to do with science than with philosophy, using that term in its broadest sense; had less to do with execution than with the definition of terms and the setting of goals.

Restoration had originated in the early sixteenth century, as a problem in preservation. Leonardo's *Last Supper* had been as much an experiment in fresco technique—in glazes and pigments and the porousness of plaster—as it had been an experiment in psychology and form. Even before it was completed, the great work had begun to disintegrate. And other, still young, acknowledged masterworks, the Paduan chapel of Giotto, for example, the Crucifix of Brunelleschi, were, by the sixteenth century, already showing signs of age, were being corrupted by leaks and drafts, by the smoke of incessantly burning candles. So there had been, at first, the varnishes—the extracts of animal and essences of plant—which, all too frequently, had accelerated the destruction of the surfaces on which they were rubbed. And even when these substances retarded deterioration, there was the unfortunate trade-off: the overall darkening, the loss of subtlety and detail, the transformation of highly colored works, with starkly contrasting passages, into works of uniform mellowness or dullness, of rich browns or lifeless grays.

Not all that much thereafter the revisions had started. Later generations, failing to fully comprehend the intentions of their ancestors, or scandalized by those intentions, or believing they could improve upon them, had begun to edit or extrapolate, to paint over what was offensive or inartfully done, as judged by contemporary standards. Michelangelo had been dead hardly a hundred years before the defiant nudes of the Sistine *Last Judgment* had been covered in loincloths. And, soon after, when it had become an article of Roman Catholic faith that mathematical perspective was part of the order of the universe, gross distortions in scale, so common in works of the Dark Ages—and reflecting an ordering of the relative religious significance of people and things— had been eliminated in favor of a system based strictly on distance from the viewer, with a steady diminution in the size of objects accompanying their recession in space.

With advances in art historical understanding and in the capacity of chemistry to determine the relative ages of pigment, and to remove the newer pigment without destroying the older, "true" restoration had commenced, an art whose aim was the restoration of paintings to their pristine state and reflecting the original intentions of their makers.

No one knew better than Jacob that tapestries, no less than frescoes and freestanding paintings, had suffered the whims of successive sets of owners: their attempts at cleaning, their incompetent patching and reweaving of loose threads, and their large-scale alterations to the pictorial content of the surfaces. Like old paintings, tapestries were multi-generational assemblages, and as with old paintings, there were limits on what the restorer could accomplish. Sometimes, Jacob reflected, it was not altogether possible to undo the damage. History too many times rewritten could destroy the past.

But in the tapestry before him, Jacob thought he could see clear to the bottom, to the years 1410 and 1411. He would begin with the figure in the left middle ground, the Count of Langenhagen.

It was an affront, a challenge that, the Count resolved, would have to be met. Here, in his own neck of the woods, there still survived a unicorn, reputedly a fierce one, which, far from evading its pursuers by dint of its superior footspeed, had met them head-on and sent them running for cover. Its presence was a personal insult, and one the Count would answer in blood. The unicorn must be destroyed, eliminated from the face of the earth, systematically tracked down, rounded up, sacrificed. The future of man depended on it. Everywhere the unicorn flourished, it fomented rebellion, unrest. It was an animal, a mere animal, a slave. But the unicorn refused to acknowledge its lowly status in the chain of being: it would not be dominated by mere mortal men; it would neither pull the plow nor permit a man to ride on its back. And worse yet, the unicorn encouraged others, by its example and its words. At night, it came and spoke in its beguiling voice, led the dogs and the horses out of their pens and stables, out into the forest, where they mingled with their wild brethren and never returned.

Men had given the unicorn its name, but still the beast ran free. And some men, failing to bring the creature to its knees, had invested it with magical, godlike qualities, had allowed it its eccentric position outside the order of things, had harbored it and kept it hidden, let it multiply until it had driven them off and claimed their territory for itself.

But the Count was going to right this wrong. He was dispensing coin all over the continent and it was having its effect. Each sighting, and the Count was off to the front, with his ferocious, obedient, hunting dogs, and he never came back unrequited. At first, he had ventured alone; now it was common for the local gentry to join him in the fray. He had the creature on the run, and its influence on its fellow beasts was nearly at an end.

His manor held evidence of countless kills: lampshades fashioned from unicorn hides, lances carved from their horns, larders full of chops and sausages saved for special feast days.

His last expedition had been particularly fruitful. In a forest far to the west, a number of woodsmen had spotted a large unicorn herd and, during a bold midnight raid, had slain a few of its number. The rest of the herd were driven to the east. By the time the caravan met the Count's party, the once-indomitable creatures, disorganized and demoralized, were spearing one another. A few arrows were all that had been required to complete the operation.

And yet, here at the other boundary of the Count's own forest, in his own back yard, was a unicorn, they said. It was an outrage.

The Count called for his dogs.

A caravan of unicorns; a cattle car of frantic passengers clacking down the track, debating what it all portended, some clawing at the doors, others sitting silently, full of hope, on their suitcases. Unforgettable, better forgotten. He had better remember. On the advice of counsel.

Jacob Altman, magnifying glass in his left hand, tweezers in his right, peered at the figure of the Count of Langenhagen, a figure unusually dense in its concentration of fiber, its threads thickly intertwined, laid one over another virtually in the manner of a soft, sculptural relief. The Count of Langenhagen, sportsman *par excellence,* so famous in his own lifetime as the fierce hunter of unicorns, was no fiercer than his companions in the hunt; if anything, Jacob mused, he was portrayed as the most pacific of the group: the red of his lips and the red that circumscribed the whites of his eyes was of a somewhat softer hue—a subtle distinction; the downturn of his mouth was a bit less pronounced; the thrust of his lance more hesitant, perhaps, as if calculated to open only a shallow incision, one that would heal successfully and leave but a small scar.

Jacob began teasing out the more recent, surface fibers, meticulously numbering them and marking their locations, and taking, at frequent intervals, scores of close-up, high-resolution photographs. It was a canon of modern restoration practice that a record be made, so that future art historians would be able to study a tapestry's afterlife, its ever-developing destiny in the hands of its successive caretakers; and in order that it should always be possible to restore a tapestry to its condition as of a previous restoration.

As Jacob Altman removed additional layers of thread, the true Count, the Count of contemporary accounts, started in Jacob's mind's eye to emerge, with lips of a fiery crimson, with cold, hard, cobalt eyes, his woven brow deeply, vertically furrowed, his right arm drawn back with a murderous potency, his upper body rippling with deadly energy. The true Count, Jacob was certain, but ultimately a threadbare Count: the original fibers of the nose were gone; of a section of the abdomen, only the underweaving, the skeleton of coarse gray thread, remained; the hand wrapped around the lance was mostly worn away. These areas, and others, Jacob would have to rework, using the fibers woven in later, the fibers he had just removed. It could be done, of that Jacob had no doubt. He had dealt in the past with tapestries far more riddled than this one.

The Count of Langenhagen, sportsman *par excellence,* so famous in his own lifetime as the ferocious hunter of unicorns, was now remembered, if at all, solely for a singular culinary achievement. In his kitchens, some scholars held, had been invented the soufflé. Of course, the Count's priority of authorship was not universally conceded. But henceforward, Jacob was confident, the Count would be remembered as the killer he had been.

[4]

They began drifting into the large conference room, Lenox's partners, Styrofoam coffeecups in hand, hastily buttoning their jackets, as you did when a new client was ushered into your office. Button with your left, shake with your right. Just like the Secretary of State greeting a foreign politico: button left, shake right. Sit down and unbutton.

After Lenox, Tilden was the first to show up, with a thick sheaf of papers, ready to take the offensive. Then Astor and Brooke, looking at their watches: time is money, ditto. Well, true to his word, he would have them back at their desks before the janitor had dumped yesterday's trash, Lenox hoped. Tilden would shoot off his mouth, let off some steam, but

Lenox could deal with him. The rest of them, Lenox hoped, would go along with whatever he said, as always. So much for law-firm democracy, the informed electorate.

When the backbenchers had made their appearance, Lenox lifted the gavel with which he called meetings to order. A gift from his daughter on the occasion of his assuming the chairmanship of the firm's executive committee. "Bang it in good health," she said. Knock on wood.

"Any of you have any suggestions?" Lenox inquired. His partners all stared blankly into space, until Tilden cleared his throat.

"I've had one of our associates looking into the Penal Code. She must've been up all night on this." Tilden waited for the nervous laughs to subside, and continued. "It seems to me that, at the least, Roland could be charged with menacing, a Class E felony. One-to-three years, with automatic expulsion from the bar. The D.A. would probably bargain it down to disorderly conduct or terroristic threat making and let him off with probation, but he still isn't going to be practicing law in this lifetime. If he doesn't have a permit, and the gun is operable, he's looking at criminal possession of a firearm in the third degree, which carries a mandatory sentence of at least a year. Considering how close he came to letting me have it, there's no reason why the D.A. couldn't charge him with assault in the first degree, or—maybe this is a bit of a stretch—attempted murder. Either way, we're talking double figures at Attica.

"The way I see it, the longer we go without reporting it, the greater the chance they'll let him off with a spanking and a 'Don't do it again.' A practical joke, a sophomore prank, they'll call it. And then when we fire him, he sues . . . civil rights, employment discrimination. We look like shit, he comes off smelling like a rose. We have to nip it in the bud, I say."

Not exactly a surprise.

What a pain in the ass Tilden was. If he didn't bring in all that business, he would be well worth buying out.

Now they were all staring into their laps, Lenox's high-powered partners. "Any other bright ideas?" Lenox looked over at Astor and Brooke sitting side by side, and nodded, too quickly to be noticed by the others. Their cue.

While attending to his urgent duties at the museum, holding their hands as they decided whether to serve cappuccino in the cafeteria, whether to display a Manet which the artist had seen fit to use as a tablecloth and which, because of its prominent coffee stains, had long ago been relegated to the museum's storage bins, Lenox had managed to devote a few moments to the "Roland affair," as it was known around the office. Lenox considered Roland, in some ways, to be a kindred spirit, and although Lenox had a business to think of, there was a part of him that wanted to shake the guy's hand, buy him a drink. It hadn't been so long since Lenox had thought about showing up for work wearing the obligatory three-piece suit, with a submachine gun tucked among the briefs in his briefcase.

Lenox had joined the firm thirty years ago, just as it was entering the modern era, the strictly-business phase. The old old-boy network was no longer enough to keep your old clients, who'd been with you since The Year One. You had to show them results, you had to get them what they wanted—by yesterday. Everything, all of a sudden, was an emergency. You needed a space-age phone system so you could talk to fifteen people at once, all over the country; and an around-the-clock secretarial pool, and a telex machine and a Xerox machine, so you could send off fifteen copies and have fifteen people going over them with a fine-toothed comb so they could get back to you in fifteen minutes. Scratch and claw to keep the old clients, wine and dine to bring in new ones—it was like a bad dream, a parody of the profession his father had labored in without ever raising a sweat.

Lenox ran his right hand along the underside of the enormous old conference table of polished walnut, feeling for the spot where, thirty years ago, after hours, he had carved his initials. There they were: J.L., and underneath: WAS HERE. Someday, maybe when the firm had grown so large that it needed a skyscraper all to itself, in the process of moving someone would overturn the table. No one would ever suspect that Lenox was the J.L. who had been there.

Lenox ran his eye along the row of portraits evenly spaced along the wall to his right. The firm's august founding fathers. If you looked closely, you could still make out the flamboyant mustaches and Van Dycks which, one, evening, Lenox had magic-markered à la Duchamp over their middle-aged likenesses. All the scrubbing that had been done had not succeeded in removing every last trace. His rookie colleagues had been in stitches for days as the managing partner, with grim inefficiency, had attempted to "get to the bottom of this outrage, this sacrilege."

The washroom's marble walls were now covered with their third or fourth layer of graffiti: boastful recordations of sexual conquests, more imagined than real, competing for space with libelous allegations concerning the sexual proclivities of despised partners, past and present. When Lenox had arrived, the walls had been bare.

Second and third mortgages, private-school tuitions, and the inevitable fading of youthful passions had all had their effect on Lenox, and he was no longer the upstart he had once been. But still, he was not the sort of parent to forget what it was like to be a kid. He'd never gone as far as Roland, not by a long shot, but Lenox knew where the guy was coming from, and if he could help it, he didn't want to see him get thrown to the dogs. He'd managed to twist a couple of arms, Astor's and Brooke's. "Just trust me on this one. I'll owe you," he'd finally had to resort to. Lenox hoped they would remember their lines.

"I beg to differ," Astor said, at last. "The paramount consideration here, I would suggest, is the continued well-

VICTOR BARALL

being of the firm. That must come first, and I hardly think that
the heavy hand of the criminal justice apparatus is what we
need at this time."

"I am constrained to agree," Brooke chimed in, right on
schedule. "While I would be the last person to welcome the
sight of the barrel of a revolver pointed in my direction, I
nonetheless believe that we must be reasoned in our response,
realizing what is at stake. We must, of necessity, therefore, find
a means to defuse the situation rather than escalate the hostilities. Surely you, Lenox, have given the matter some thought."

So far, so good.

"How could I not?" Lenox jumped in. "Naturally, I share
Tilden's view that this is the sort of thing that can't be toler-
ated, but I agree that we have more to think about than retri-
bution. From where I sit, I can see three problems that we've
got to deal with."

Listening to himself speak, glancing over the table at his
quiescent colleagues, Lenox knew that this was going to be a
breeze, a piece of cake. He had trotted out his most profes-
sorial tone and they, like college sophomores, were busy taking notes on their legal pads: (1), (2), (3), they wrote, and now
they were waiting.

"First of all, we have to come to terms with the fact that
Roland isn't alone out there in wanting to take up arms
against us. The other associates may not have the whatever-
it-takes to protest, but you can bet when they go home at
night—if they get to go home—they're busy having murderous thoughts. Roland isn't a hero for nothing, and the last
thing we need is to make a martyr out of him. So, whatever
we do, it has to be something to cool them out, rather than
fire them up. Let's not forget who does ninety percent of the
work around here.

"Second, there's Roland himself. Sure, we can send him
off to jail, but we all know that he's savvy enough to take us
with him. He makes a stink, and we're stuck with a reputation
on the street as the place to avoid at all costs, the firm that

drives its associates to the brink of insanity. We'll be lucky to get anyone to sign up for interviews. I don't think we want that.

"On the other hand, we have to work here too, and we have to be able to tell these kids what to do without getting into a debate with them whether they're going to do it or not. That, for those of you keeping count, is number three: we have to find a way to save face, to re-establish our authority without seeming to be authoritarian about it.

"So those, as I see them, are the issues, and now, how do we address them? I think Tilden may have hit on something. Suppose we were to treat this Class E felony as if it were, in fact, a schoolyard prank. Everybody wins. The associates see how reasonable we are, that we know how to take a joke, that we're not a bunch of monsters, and they're ready to get back to work, knowing that we're the only law firm in town where one's individuality is respected. That's all they need out of this.

"And if we treat it as a joke," Lenox continued, "rather than as a challenge, a threat, we don't have to call in the Marines to restore order. It was nothing, and we're still in charge, in all our benevolence.

"And then there's Roland: what's he got to complain about? He got to have his fun, and no one took him to task for it. He has a new lease on life and a whole new outlook, and we get to keep a good lawyer in the bargain. Something for everyone, like I said.

"Let me talk to him, smooth it all over, talk him out of any lingering doubts or hostilities he may be having. Meanwhile, the rest of you, you can put some color back in your faces, and go out there and let them know that they weren't the only ones who had a good laugh over Tilden dropping a load in his trousers. You told them about that, didn't you, Bill?" One of the oil paintings grinned down at Lenox.

"All right. Anyone else have anything to say about this mess?" Lenox could hear Tilden grumbling under his breath—a bunch of pantywaists, Tilden was calling his colleagues. Pantywaists? Lenox had never heard that one before. "Bill, what do you say?"

Tilden stopped his muttering. "Obviously I don't have the votes, after such a stirring speech, such a demonstration of hypothetico-deductive reasoning. Who am I, next to Socrates? Or is it Neville Chamberlain?"

No need to respond. Let Tilden get in a few cracks, Lenox reasoned. "All right, then. A show of hands? Okay. Let's get out there and bill some hours and kick some ass."

Lenox lowered his gavel. Meeting adjourned.

[5]

Unicorn tapestries, such as the one on which Jacob was now working, had once, for a brief period, been very much in vogue as wedding presents, accompanying the bride out of the chapel and into the unfamiliar castle of the groom. It was Jacob who had first made the connection between the genre and the joinder of sons with daughters. Inspired by his investigations into the meaning of the family emblems on this particular set of tapestries, a number of art historians had begun to explore the circumstances surrounding the commissioning of other surviving unicorn tapestry specimens. In several cases, they had uncovered unimpeachable evidence to link the surfacing of a member of the exotic, one-horned species with a mating between two powerful families. Records in the British Museum, for example, revealed that such a series had made the voyage to England with Margaret of Anjou, the wife of Henry VI. The lack of finish and the carelessness of execution perhaps reflected the haste with which the marriage had been contracted.

The Passion of the Unicorn, Jacob had persuasively argued, was a fitting symbol for the tying of the marriage knot: just as the unicorn, the lord of the forest, so solitary and wild, was surrounded, taunted, and stabbed, carried off defeated to be laid at the feet of a beautiful innocent, a creature with no sin; so, too, the young bachelor, lorded over by no one, was required by the community of men to give up his carefree existence and answer the call of home and hearth, to rein in his profane appetites and—at least as a matter of aspiration, if not of actual practice—confine his carnal attentions to the sanctified body of his one rightful companion on earth. Of course, Jacob knew, not every unicorn tapestry was susceptible to this interpretation. The Unicorns in the Cluny, whose history was well documented, had commemorated no temporal union; rather, those tapestries had been meant to symbolize the Passion of Christ and, so far as anyone could tell, that sequence of events only.

That the unicorn, during its several-hundred-year appearance in Western art, had been equated with the Christ was a nineteenth-century insight: the art historians Burckhardt and Wölfflin had each, in passing, made reference to the possibility of devoting a monograph to the subject, but neither had progressed beyond a preliminary handwritten draft; Pater, however, had taken up the suggestion and produced a lengthy essay which, in turn, had formed the basis for the more rigorous—and in the opinion of many, the definitive—treatment by Benjamin. According to Benjamin, there was a striking similarity between the character and fate of the Son of God and the character and fate of the unicorn, as developed in every known tapestry series. If the Christ was God's only begotten Son, and was the only being to possess a dual nature—at once human in form and divine in spirit—the unicorn also was a singular creature, always depicted alone, as if it were the only member of its species; and the unicorn, by virtue of the widely-held skepticism that it truly existed, was an entity corporeal in form but perhaps actually residing only in the human imagination—the frail human correlate of divine creativity, of pure spirit. The horrendous destruction of the Christ by Caesar's centurions; the quiet suffering of the Virgin, cradling her dead son in her lap; and the wondrous emergence of the Christ from His Tomb all found their parallels in the story of the unicorn: its unnatural death, its somber presentation to a spot-less maiden, and its strange rebirth.

It followed, Benjamin had reasoned, that the supporting actors in the unicorn drama should be assigned roles corre-sponding to the functions of their analogues in the Gospel accounts: the regal hunters—who, by the penultimate frame, were not so proud of their deed—should be seen as the be-nighted citizens of Rome, who, it was true, slew their Saviour, but who, noble enough to perceive their error, soon accepted him as such; and the dogs—who never relented in their taste for blood—should be seen as the Jews, who, without apology, without repentance, unleashed their fury on one of their own and never looked back.

That, in essence, was Benjamin's thesis. Contrary to the allegations of certain scholars—Jew haters, all of them, Jacob believed, who plainly did not want a Jew looking into, tamper-ing with, their sacred images—Jacob had never downplayed, let alone denied, the religious significance of the unicorn tapestries. *Ad hominem* attacks, willful obfuscations, wanton misreadings of his work—that is all these charges amounted to. In truth, Jacob, by bringing to light the historical context of these works, had merely sought to expand the body of knowledge concerning them. After all, there was no incompat-ibility, no reason why the two symbologies could not coexist: marriage, in Christian terms, was a sacred union only insofar as it was presided over by the earthly representatives of Christ, and celebrated the mystic wedding of Christ and the Church. Indeed, it was the theological significance of the Encounter tapestry that, at the moment, was Jacob's exclusive interest.

Having completed the figure of the Count of Langenha-gen, Jacob set to work on the Count's son, next over to the right, a hateful young man, a veritable Hitler Youth type, cut from the same cloth as his father but lacking the father's diabolical genius. Having watched his father eradicate the uni-corn population of Europe, the son had embarked on a mission no less sadistic, if numerically far more difficult: it was to the son that the upper classes' mania for fox hunting could be traced. His image required little effort on Jacob's part: neither the original patron nor later generations had expended a great deal of polemical energy on the son, and the threads that formed him were among the best preserved in the entire work.

Moving along to the right, Jacob considered the figure of the Margrave of Stadthagen.

It mattered little, one way or the other. If the Count of Langenhagen had such a deep conviction, such a strong grievance, that he believed the unicorn had to be resettled elsewhere, outside the wood running between their properties, there was no reason to dispute him. It was not as if the unicorn would rise to the Margrave's defense were the tables turned.

Why stick his neck out? The Count was hardly someone you could persuade with logical argument. The two of them had coexisted peaceably these last twenty years. Why play with fire? The Count, were he so inclined, could vanquish him in a moment, overrun his lands with his vassals and those vicious dogs that he had been breeding nonstop. It was better to go along. He had nothing against the unicorn, but he could live just as comfortably, more comfortably, were it somewhere else.

The Count had directed the Margrave to keep watch over the forest for unicorns, and he had sighted one. Barricades he had constructed kept it from straying too far afield. He would notify the Count. So be it. Let the Creator worry about the fate of His creatures; let Him separate the dead from the quick, if it came to that.

After forty days and forty nights, Noah had unbolted the door and extended a narrow beam across to dry earth, the Margrave recalled from Scripture, and some of His original creations, not equal to the task, too weak from the voyage to plant a firm step, had fallen into the sea. That was His will, not Noah's failing.

The door slid open, creaking along its runners; the faint, exhausted passengers picked up their baggage and disembarked, some staggering, falling, gasping for breath; some others, with deeper reserves of strength, emerging almost intact. Jacob felt on his wrist the sting of a baton, directing him and his wife to one side, and saw others, his brother, similarly stung, lining up to the other.

The Margrave of Stadthagen had gone for centuries without the slightest alteration. But then, immediately following the Second World War, a team of French restorers—without otherwise reworking the tapestry in any material respect—had effected a major change in the figure of the Margrave. As he now stood, the Margrave could do no harm to any creature in the landscape: the path that his spear would travel once it left his raised arm led only into the unpopulated undergrowth. The French restorers, acting on the basis of no evidence that Jacob was aware of, had completely woven over the antique spear and replaced it with a spear of their own devising. Jacob snipped and discarded the postwar threads to reveal, underneath, the original instrument of warfare, whose trajectory led straight to the heart of the unicorn. It was the Margrave, as it were, who, from the pathologist's standpoint at least, had hurled the fatal strike, dealt the deadly blow.

[6]

Lenox hadn't used the letter opener in years. Another whimsical gift from his whimsical daughter. Ivory handle and silver blade, the latter engraved with a spurious aphorism purporting to be the final judgment of that old Civil War veteran Oliver Wendell Holmes, arrived at after a life on the bench, carving out the Rule of Law: "The sword is mightier than the pen." On his tearing open the wrapping, Lenox's daughter had challenged him: "Just try opening a package with a ballpoint some time and you'll see that he was right."

Lenox hadn't had much occasion lately to use either pen or prize sword. Clients, it seems, were suing their lawyers these days right and left, at the drop of a hat. At the insistence of the law firm's malpractice insurance carrier, every *i* had to be dotted, every *t* crossed, every stone overturned, every ass covered, no skeleton left rattling, which also meant that every piece of his correspondence had to be opened and stamped—RECEIVED, with the date—before it was entrusted to Lenox. That RECEIVED stamp had cost Lenox a couple of pretty good mementoes: a handwritten note from the Chief Justice thanking him for serving on the Federal Rules Revision Committee, an out-of-the-blue proclamation from the Mayor recognizing his lifelong contributions to the "quality of life" in the city— whatever that meant. RECEIVED, RECEIVED. No longer suitable for framing. Well, he shouldn't get a swelled head anyway.

While she was at it, defacing his mail, Lenox's hyperefficient secretary, on her own notion, had taken to sorting it as well. It took the joy out of Lenox's first hour in the office, to have his mail pre-read, but, he guessed, he shouldn't complain: his time was too valuable. Time is money. Time is money. The pile of papers on the far left pertained to cases Lenox was working on: letters from clients, outlandish demands from adversaries, orders from various judges flexing their judicial muscles inside those black robes. Next over, law firm business: interoffice memos, checks needing his signature. In the middle pile, bar association activities: committee meetings, guest lectures at area law schools, etc. Then, charities wanting money; and on the far right, the new pile: art museum business. He'd get to that in a moment. First, the worthy causes.

Being a pillar of the community, so-called, carried a high price tag. Organizations these days could bring in a few bucks selling their mailing lists to other organizations, and Lenox's name had certainly been making the rounds. He was averaging fifteen solicitations a day, but today he'd gotten off easy: only five dire pleas for critically needed funds.

It was a wonder anyone ever lived to a ripe old age with all the diseases out there. The National Lupus Foundation claimed that researchers were close to a cure—but they needed his help. The March of Dimes, with more bravado than real hope, was determined to do away with birth defects by the start of the next century. The Anti-Vivisection League, however, had sent a color photograph of a shrieking monkey bound to some piece of equipment, and called for a moratorium on medical research while its lawsuit challenging the constitutionality of animal experimentation worked its way through the courts. The Women's Christian Temperance Union, Lenox read with some disbelief, was making a comeback, and its Political Action Fund had targeted several hard-drinking senators for eviction from the Congress. Last, the Mikva Institute for Eastern European Studies had in mind an oral-history project of immense proportions: they wanted to record the life story of every single person born east of the Rhine who had emigrated to the United States before 1950. Death or fading memories would soon silence these voices forever. The time to act was now. Or never. Lenox buzzed his secretary: "Helen, could you find out if I have any money in checking?"

Lenox gingerly fingered the Urgent—underlined twice— Request for Intervention from the curator of Late Medieval Art. What now?

Altman, the curator reported, had run amok. Unless, of course, he hadn't: the curator couldn't make up his mind. He had visited Altman's workshop to check on the progress of the tapestry, which was taking a little longer than had been hoped, considering how many people the work drew into the museum at $5 a pop. But you couldn't rush Altman, and the curator hadn't intended to; he had just wanted to see how far along things were.

The workshop had been somewhat of a shock. Tables were piled high with bales of old thread, strangely labeled: *Count L.—First Fabrication; Count L.—Second Fabrication; Count L.—Most Recent Fabrication.* Meanwhile, the tapestry itself, famous the world over for the lushness of its fiber, the luxuriant density of its surface, had been reduced to a still vivid, but thinly woven, work of art. And what's more, the curator said, faces had been changed, postures changed, roles reversed, everything had been turned inside out.

This didn't mean, the curator told Lenox, that Altman's conception was necessarily off the mark: Altman certainly knew a lot more about this stuff than anyone else out there—although, given the look of things in the workshop, one could not be completely confident that Altman was on target, either. But in any event, the curator hastened to add, whether Altman had truly recaptured the tapestry as it had originally appeared or had simply gone off the deep end was, to a degree—an important degree—beside the point.

For centuries, the curator supposed, people had been looking at the tapestry as it had appeared before Altman started unraveling it, and had lived their lives accordingly, absorbing its messages and, based on those messages, formulating images of the world. Was it appropriate, the curator pondered, to simply discard a set of meanings which had developed over centuries, in favor of the original text? The tapestry, after all, no longer belonged to its patron; it belonged to the world.

Suppose, the curator ventured by way of illustration, one day we were to discover that, contrary to long-held belief, the sun revolved around the earth or, for that matter, that Jesus had never walked on the face of the earth. What would be the consequences of publishing such intelligence? "Please think about it," the curator implored Lenox, "and go have a look for yourself."

Well, Lenox most certainly would think about it, let it percolate through his brain along with the morning's first cup of coffee. Maybe he'd even make a field trip, take the afternoon off. Meanwhile, Roland was waiting in his outer office.

"Come on in, make yourself comfortable," Lenox beckoned to Roland. "Let me just go through a few of these bills and I'll be right with you."

Roland didn't look too good, Lenox noticed. None of the associates looked too good. Not enough sleep, not enough exercise, living on fast food—they were all a little flabby, pasty-faced, bloodshot in the eyes; their clothes were always a little rumpled. Roland had kept up appearances a little better—he must have been one of the associates who had registered his measurements with Brooks Brothers so that if he didn't get home at night he could still have a fresh shirt in the morning, delivered to the office by 9 A.M. He must have hundreds of white shirts, worn only once, hanging in his closet. But today he looked as disheveled as the rest.

"Roland, I just wanted to clear the air. These past few weeks, I figure you've been waiting for the other shoe to drop."

"Yes, sir."

Roland murmured so softly. He barely made eye contact.

"I want you to know: you have nothing to worry about. We're not going to press charges, we're not going to fire you."

Now Roland met him with an icy, penetrating stare. "Hey look, Mr. Lenox, don't do me any favors."

"Who said anything about favors? Believe me, this has nothing to do with Christian charity: I'm doing this for my-self."

Damn. Roland wasn't buying any of it. Still staring that icy stare.

"Let me tell you a story, Mr. Lenox, a little something you wouldn't know. Perhaps it'll change your mind."

What the hell did Roland want, Lenox wondered.

"At the Harvard Law School, my first year there, there was a certain someone who got into the habit of setting fire to the law dorms. At all hours of the day or night, students would discover these minor conflagrations, burning in stairwells or trash cans. Not exactly roaring fires such as might result in loss of life—just petty, unprovoked acts of vandalism, easily extinguished, but leaving behind an odor of smoke and a fear of what was next to come. Suspicion, naturally, fell on the janitorial staff. Only the roommate of this certain someone knew the identity of the guilty party, and he would not speak.

"Early one morning, just before the start of final exams, a succession of stones was hurled through the windows of Langdell Hall. The roommate finally went to the Dean. The perpetrator, with the Dean's most sincere apologies, was suspended for a semester, returned, graduated with honors, and went to work at a prestigious law firm. The roommate, meanwhile, owing to his lack of solidarity with the oppressed, has been a pariah among his classmates ever since. I'm sure, by now, you have figured out who this certain someone was, Mr. Lenox."

He was supposed to be unflappable, supposedly he never batted an eye at anything, but Lenox had to admit it to himself: he was a little rattled, just a little, but not enough to weaken his resolve. He would stick to his guns.

"Helen, hold my calls," he whispered over the intercom. "Roland, is that all? That's it? I hear you, and to tell you the truth, I don't care. In our profession, and outside our profession, people with a little heart are harder and harder to find. You are a vanishing breed, an endangered species. And besides that, this firm can use a shaking up from time to time."

Roland was melting, a little tear hung at the corner of his right eye. "Have it your way, Mr. Lenox. But remember, from now on, you are an aider and abettor, a collaborator, in whatever might happen."

Empty threats, spoken too softly to be backed by conviction.

"I'll take my chances," Lenox responded.

VICTOR BARALL

[7]

Less than a week before Jacob Altman commenced
work on the tapestry, he received a subpoena directing that he
appear for a hearing in Courtroom 3B, United States District
Court, Foley Square, said hearing to commence six weeks,
forty days, from the date of the subpoena. The hearing was on
Jacob's mind as he commenced work, like a dripping faucet,
like a fly buzzing around his ear, like a perplexing dream from
the night before, like a sword of Damocles.

According to the Complaint accompanying the subpoena,
one Hyman Felderman, a survivor of the *Lager* at Theresienstadt, riding on a crosstown bus, had instantly recognized
Jacob seated across the aisle, had exited behind him, and,
following him to his apartment house, had recorded his
address.

Each barracks in the camp, according to Mr. Felderman,
had been administered by an inmate commandant upon whom
devolved the responsibility, among others, of selecting
each day a number of persons to be sent to the gas chambers.
Jacob Altman had been the commandant of Mr. Felderman's
barracks.

Typically, inmates were chosen for the position arbitrarily,
generally against their will, and, not atypically, chose themselves for death rather than persevere in the hellish task. It was
believed, by Mr. Felderman at least, that Altman had volunteered for the assignment, and according to Mr. Felderman, if
no one else, Altman could be brutal with those who lagged in
their work and who, Altman had said, threatened the survival
of them all. Mr. Felderman claimed to have personally felt on
one occasion the sting of Altman's whip and claimed to have
seen others whipped also.

What, Jacob asked himself, could this Felderman possibly
know about it, why he had done it, what it had cost him? For
his wife—they had promised him his wife if he did it. But they
had not kept their word.

189

On applying for permanent resident status, the Complaint alleged, and on applying for citizenship, Jacob Altman had willfully misrepresented himself to the immigration authorities. He had stated, under oath, that he had been interned at Theresienstadt, which was true enough, but he had failed to disclose what he had done there. A lie by omission, the Complaint said, the penalty for which, if the allegations were well-founded, was the revocation of citizenship.

As Jacob commenced work on the dogs, the hearing was but one week away.

When, around the turn of the century, Benjamin, the definitive monographist, described the dogs in Jacob's tapestry as entirely consistent with the representations of hunting dogs in other unicorn tapestries, he could not have realized that he was mistaken. Never having traveled to the United States, Benjamin had to have based his observations on the set of dim black-and-white photographs that the museum was then disseminating among serious scholars, photographs which scarcely did justice to the tapestries in all their plethora of detail. But that was not Benjamin's only handicap: even if he had chanced to venture to America, he might well have arrived at the same, mistaken conclusion, inasmuch as the dogs, along with so much else, had been so insistently altered long before his day. It would have taken a well-trained restorer, rather than a mere amateur art historian—albeit a most insightful and reliable one such as Benjamin—to have been capable of sifting through the fibers to see the dogs in their earliest manifestation. Benjamin's error, therefore, was entirely understandable and, in Jacob's opinion, was not one Benjamin could be faulted for.

But Jacob, by contrast, would have been remiss had he failed to perceive the changes that had been wrought. Indeed, he reflected, perhaps he had already been remiss, for on the several prior occasions he had been commissioned to refurbish the tapestry, he had not been struck by anything out of the ordinary in the dogs. Now, however, the alterations, although subtle, seemed to Jacob unmistakable.

With the removal of each layer of threads there was reduced the dogs' level of viciousness: bared teeth receded into mouths, throaty barking and snarling subsided into the yelps of plaintive greeting, tails lifted in excited anticipation lowered and fell between hind legs. The dogs, when Jacob was through with them—when he had removed the fibers of revision and filled in the gaps, the lost passages: when he had deduced from what remained that which had to have been—when Jacob was through with them, the dogs could only be described as a somber, pacific group; one dog in particular, outdoing the rest, actually lay on its back, paw raised, neck exposed, in a posture of surrender. From a religious standpoint, the previously obscured message of the tapestry had become clear: the Jews, the original tapestry had proclaimed, were not responsible, could not be held accountable, for the destruction of their fellow worshipper, their so-called King. But if this judgment had only recently, and at that, only halfheartedly, been accepted in Rome, how, Jacob wondered, in the depths of darkest Germany, the last place on earth, could such an idea have developed?

Jacob considered the lone remaining human figure, the figure he had not yet touched, the Duke of Hannover—the father-in-law, the patron of the work, according to whose instructions it had been executed; and Jacob considered the unicorn, with its all-too-human face.

The marriage that the tapestry commemorated, Jacob knew, was not fated to be a long one, and it had produced not a single heir. The groom, Felix the Pious, had perished in 1412, less than a year following the wedding; a victim, if church records could be trusted, of an epidemic of the plague. Not all his wealth could save him. His premature death, one might suggest with a slight bow in the direction of the supernatural, had been foretold in the tapestry, for the unicorn's countenance, which bore Felix's likeness, displayed more than the usual measure of pain appropriate to a dying beast, a retiring bachelor, or a Man of Sorrows. Jacob discerned in the face of the creature a special poignancy, a specific gaze absent from the unicorns in all other tapestries and bespeaking a particularized awareness of the earthly mortality to come.

The Duke of Hannover, according to the church records Jacob had studied, had likewise perished in 1412, falling in the path of the same omnivorous bacillus which, in 1410, had already claimed the lives of so many. At some point not long after the Duke's death, the illustrious tapestry series had passed into the hands of the Count of Langenhagen.

The Duke of Hannover, as he stood before Jacob, was, without a doubt, the villain of the piece. It was he who evinced the strongest hatred, the most complete antipathy to the luckless animal: a shadow blackened his brow, a scowl passed across his lips; his spear he raised with the most evil of intents, and his aim was true. This representation, Jacob intuited, could not have been what the patron had ordered. Vanity alone would have prevented the Duke from having himself so depicted, as would the circumstances of the commission: would a father-in-law give such a gift to his eldest daughter's husband-to-be? And then there were the other figures, all of whom had undergone some revision or other over the course of time.

Jacob pulled from his toolbox tools he had not used, he thought, for decades: wire cutters, crochet needles, large sewing shears, tools lacking in tact, tools unsuitable for delicate operations but suitable, it seemed to Jacob, for this one. He attacked the tapestry with an abandon, with an ecstasy he had not known since his youth. The new Duke, the old Duke, rapidly emerged from beneath the ropes that had bound him.

"Stop," he cried, "stop. No more of this, enough." His

arms, weaponless, were spread wide, his spread fingers begged for mercy, his eyes rose heavenward. An impotent, would-be protector, around whom the lances, the heedless arrows flew.

When, more than thirty years earlier, Jacob had first noted the coats of arms on the museum's tapestries and had been drawn into the church records of Lower Saxony—the baptismal certificates, marriage certificates, death certificates, the census records for the years 1410, 1411, 1412—he had not failed to notice the two outbreaks of the plague, and he had been struck by the names of the plague victims. If Jacob's recollections served him, overwhelmingly they were Jewish-sounding names, he recalled, names like Judah and Elijah and Saul. And among the victims for the year 1412, the Duke of Hannover and Felix the Pious.

Felix the Pious, if his name meant anything, was as good a Christian as the next, but, Jacob knew, Felix had not always been a Christian. His great-grandfather Moses the Pious had been a talmudic scholar and a moneylender of some prominence; his grandfather, however, had converted to the true faith, and Felix, and his father before him, had been baptized in that faith.

Jacob knew he could not prove it, but he doubted that the plague was the true cause of all these deaths that had been so faithfully recorded in the records of the region. The tapestry told him otherwise. The denizens of Lower Saxony, Jacob surmised, had been infested with a plague of Jews and, accordingly, had resolved to wage a war against them, to unleash a plague on the parasites. The Duke, for reasons that would forever be secret, had been mortified and, glimpsing the future, grasping what was still to come, had thought that if Felix were his son-in-law, he could save him. But once a Jew, always a Jew: the sins of the fathers shall be visited on the sons, for generations and generations, *in saecula, saeculorum*. The Duke, hopelessly overmatched, could not save Felix; the fool, he could only perish with him.

The lawyer from the Justice Department was making his closing statement, summing up the evidence against Jacob Altman, and Jacob could not believe what he was hearing. "For too long," the lawyer said, "we as a society have looked the other way, allowed these war criminals to alter their identities and flourish right here in our midst. But the time has come to expose these Nazis and their henchmen, to flush them from the woodwork, to remove them from the fabric of American society."

How, Jacob wondered, could this be said without those in the room breaking into laughter at the hypocrisy of it all? With all those Nazis out there, why were they coming after Jews? How could it be? Next, they would be saying there were no Nazis, no camps, that it was all a Jewish plot.

And now—didn't it just take the cake?—the lawyer was invoking the words of the great Jewish jurist: "As Felix Frankfurter put it so well, 'Wisdom too often never comes, and so one ought not to reject it merely because it comes late.'"

On March 31, 1988, Jacob Altman completed his restoration. The following day, Good Friday, it was ordered that he be deported.

[8]

When Lenox walked into his office—his own office—Tilden was already there, sitting behind his desk. If there was one thing Lenox couldn't stand, that was it, and Tilden knew it.

"John, I've been waiting for you," Tilden bellowed gleefully.

"Bill, what do you want?"

"I realized I had to go over your head. Get a load of this."

Tilden handed him a couple of sheets of paper—an indictment, the highest count of which charged attempted murder. How in hell had Tilden managed to talk the D.A. into that?

"Bill, get the hell out of my chair."

Tilden wasn't budging, and so Lenox grabbed his gavel. "Bill, I mean it."

Tilden—the coward—dashed by him out the door.

There was a letter from the chairman of the Board of Trustees. The Late Medieval curator, apparently, had also gone over Lenox's head. It had been decided that the full board would take up the matter of the tapestry. In view of Mr. Altman's suspect motivations, the letter said, this restoration could not be accorded the same degree of deference that his work had enjoyed in the past.

It wasn't going to be Lenox's day. He ticked off in his mind all the things that could yet go wrong. He was not a man given to ordinary superstition; experience, however, had taught him that bad luck, like the faces of God, came in threes. **Q**

I Am Not So Old

The snow had been falling all over and into itself.
Everything was getting whiter and lighter and cleaner. Everything will be fine, Harry had thought on the way to the hospital, but now the sun was behind the clouds and was warming
the snow to rain and everything that was white and light and
clean was gray and heavy and muddy and Harry was saying,
"Another, please," and looking out the window at the two
women who were crossing the street. He liked their little steps
and their short coats and the way their arms folded hugging
their breasts and when they turned the corner just in front of
the bar he leaned forward, pressing his forehead against the
glass to see if he could see more.

"Don't strain your neck, Harry," said the waitress, who
was Celia.

Harry sat down and looked at his hands and saw Celia's
hand with a beer appear. Then he saw Celia standing there,
hovering. "How old are you, Celia?" Harry said.

"Thirty-four."

He looked up and saw her eyes and the red rouge under
them.

"Is there something in my hair?" Celia said.

"No," said Harry. "How many beers have I had, Celia?"
said Harry.

"This is your fifth," the waitress said.

When he had come in and it had been snowing, the beer
was golden or amber or just like how they say it is on the TV,
but now it was yellow and Harry wished there were more foam
from it on top.

Die Blume they called the foam in Germany. *La fleur* they
called the foam in France. The flower they called it. But Harry
never got it with Celia because Celia was always trying to give

Harry more beer and less foam. So Harry figured Celia did not know what the Germans and the French did.

"How old do you think those two were?" Harry said.

Celia winked and walked away.

"Hey, Celia!" Harry called.

Celia looked at him from across the bar.

"How old do you think I am, Celia?"

"My age?" the waitress said.

Harry didn't say anything but sat and drank from his beer.

"So how old are you, Harry?" the waitress said.

"Your age," Harry said.

He drank again and spread his hands flat on the table. Nicks and cuts marked his knuckles and he started picking at a splinter in the heel of his hand.

"What're you doing here, anyway?" the waitress said.

"Just felt like having a beer," Harry said.

"I thought maybe you had something in mind," the waitress said.

"Nothing in mind," Harry said.

"Are you all right?" the waitress said.

"Sure, I'm all right," Harry said.

Harry drank down his beer, lifting his glass high so Celia would know he was finished.

Celia said, "You want another one?"

Harry said he wanted another one, and the waitress brought over two beers, one for her and one for Harry. The beers came yellow and with no foam on them. Harry held up his glass and said, "Die Blume, la fleur, the flower." Harry said, "There is a street in Paris on the bank of this river, and the stores are so nice on this street, sort of like the Meadowood Mall, only not like it. They have all the newest things, whatever you could think of, all of them so different and selling different things. Hell, they sell everything. Not like here. And there's this stuff, which is like liver but not like any liver we have. Sort of soft, and tastes great, and sometimes it has these things in it. It tastes so good you think you could eat it forever but you can't eat it forever because it tastes too good. And when the smells come out of the bakeries, even if it's just bread, you feel like you have to eat it. You can smell everything from far away. And you don't have to go back to your room and turn on the TV to watch some stupid thing or the news. You could just stay out and never do anything else. You could walk around and watch the light change until it got dark out. You could walk around in some new linen skirt you bought because that is what women wear there, and maybe a sweater sometimes because it's always nice out and never hot like here. You could walk. You could watch. You could just sit somewhere. Then when it starts getting dark and the white stone isn't so white anymore, you can go to where the lights are coming on. The lights there are always coming on."

"Oh, Harry," the waitress said.

"You are so pretty, Celia," Harry said.

He moved and knocked over his beer with his elbow. He leaned over the spilled beer and kissed her.

She said, "Oh, Harry."

Harry was trying to kiss her again. So she moved her head and let him kiss her neck. Harry thought he might be getting sick, but he only belched a little under his breath.

"What?" he said, without knowing he said what or what to or even that he was speaking or she was at all. There was only suddenly her neck and below that her breast and below that the stomach and below that was that—which was what he thought he wanted.

"Mmmm," he said, and tried to touch her breast.

The waitress said, "There are people." She said, "We aren't in Paris yet."

His fingers folded into fists and he stared straight into the spilled beer.

"You're just like her," he said.

"Her?" the waitress said.

"At the hospital," Harry said.

"Now?" the waitress said.

"Now," Harry said.

"You bastard," the waitress said.

She leaned away abruptly and hit Harry in the face and screamed, "You fucking bastard!"

Harry's eyes watered and some blood was on his lip. He didn't wipe it off but could taste it and it tasted like her and like the baby to him.

He said, "Okay."

Everything will be okay, he thought, getting up and getting into his coat. He could see that rain was falling now. There is still time, he thought. Anything is possible. I am not so old, he thought. **Q**

Cyreniad

I wanted nothing more to do
with him than any other Jew,
true to Moses and the prophets.
     Yet they made me

carry his cross. By God, I have
been damned! I cried. What now can save
me from my complicity, I
     who was their slave

till the mallets fell? Afterward,
I forsook the feast and turned toward
home before evening, forgetting
     his muttered words,

his blood, that Roman excrement.
—I have my groves, and am content.

Editors: A Bestiary

Like monkeys
they pick each other's scalps
for lice.

They go on all four like dogs
and lick each other's asses
for leftovers.

Giraffes are more sorry
they have no voices
to say what they really mean.

Like donkeys under the whip,
refusing to budge,
they wish they could be human.

The News & World Report

A body was found today,
not the body we thought originally,
but another, also dead.

Hunger, About It

Hunger. Think about it. Imagine
a big man; by big
I mean bigger than you;
a man carrying a bagful of doughnuts;
by bagful I mean two dozen
or so; a man walking toward his car;
by car I mean one with some rust
on the body; a man walking at 4 A.M.,
or thereabouts, walking early,
before the birds at least,
before black coffee, but thinking
about it, about hunger, that is.

10:20

It was 10:20
all day the day
he ran over the dog.

Canned Laughter

Every time
we drink
together.

Real or Unreal Pancake Syrup

It's not real
unless you ask
for it, says
the waitress.

The World for Raym

It is either too big,
or too small, or not
for sale.

How to Find God

Go to a library.
Ask directions.

STEPHEN HICKOFF

Soul

Soul,
fillet o'
soul,
when you
go, you
go.

Miss Like

I like to go camping and like
when it gets real cold.
I like to put a sweater on and
like curl up and stuff.

It's a Plastic Wedding Cake

he said.
Nobody uses a real cake
anymore.
This is the '80s, man.
Hey,
trust me.
I'm no photographer
for nothing.

Paris Fashions

will be hotter than ever
when the UFOs come.

The Island

What Gauguin heard on the beach at Mataiea
was the voice of the planet out along the reef.
He lit a cigarette and looked away
toward the great black mountain. Where his life
had driven him thus far was nowhere near
as long from home as he was doomed to be,
though far enough for now. The mountain wore
what seemed to him a face of irony,
as if the answer to the question was
an altogether different kind of question
about the body being what it is—
an island in the middle of an ocean
moaning beyond its cold periphery
against the violet tedium of the sky.

The Dream Vacation

We leave the children at their uncle's place,
live for two weeks on the train from London
to Istanbul and back, by way of Paris,
Munich, Vienna, Budapest, and Athens,
including a sea voyage down to Crete
to sit on Minos's alabaster throne,
the locusts roaring in a door of light,
the dusty bus back to Iráklion,
an empty wine bottle thrown in the ship's wake,
Piraeus by dawn, the second-class coach at noon.

The children, at the uncle's pleasure palace,
learn to play blackjack with his lady friend.
She's glad to be with someone else's kids.
The days flow by around the swimming pool.
He brings home pizza, videos, Diet Coke.
The privacy fence keeps water like a jewel
and leaping bodies, while the sky above
is the same sky that covers the Aegean
in the other life all of us go on living,
by pools of light, in bodies lit with love.

The Banquet

A hallway bigger than most people's houses
awaited me in the next-to-last episode.
At the end of it a massive double door
opened on the Duke of Tuscany at table
attended by naked dwarfs. I stayed outside
to watch the evening play through the draperies
at the farther end of the hall where I came from,
with its enormous doorways quiet as caverns.
I knew there were councillors in the anteroom
full of news even I could deliver with aplomb,
but the lord was at table in the midst of his joy,
made much of, whispered to, kept in regard
by persons whose bodies fed from his own.
Behind me other doors were wobbling shut.
I knew if I walked in to where the great man was,
my soul no longer would be mine to save.
Glory and madness dwelt in the one room.
The way my shoulders turned when I looked back
was like a wall that stood behind my eyes
and echoed with the good loud noise I made.

Off I-70

This is the way the mind moves back.
This is the wind rippling long stands
of grassland and corn, lifting quickly
each blade's lighter shade.
All day along the highway, the fields
flickered their degree of green, shadows
only half hidden amid stalk and leaf;
this lasted for miles. How could I
think only of you, your tight, pale face,
and your eyes, your hand waving and waving
while I drove away?

A little girl stands by the motel pool,
waving her arms above the water.
She watches the surface
and beneath the surface,
then laughs and jumps in. For a moment
she floats face down, and I know
she is watching her shadow
play along the bottom, her delicate ripple
of arms and legs, light
making the limbs look thin as bones.
And I am thinking of Ben,

of how all that summer he moved through the camp
as if it was not real. I was nineteen,
had never seen children like this:
the girl whose brother raped her
mornings before school, the boy whose mother's lover
beat her while her children watched. And Ben,
knocked senseless by his father

the week before Easter.
His hair was cut so short it shimmered
the way coals do, or wheat in the wind
a long way off. We touched him as much
and often as we could, until sometimes, after
    supper,
he would come to sit in someone's lap, quiet,
leaning his head back, looking at nothing.

As the sun dips behind buildings,
the girl's mother sits up,
adjusts her bathing suit. Her daughter
hugs a towel tightly to her chest and shivers,
safe and impatient. Soon
they have gathered their things
and left—back to the room to shower
and dress for dinner, wake the girl's father,
put everything into its rhythm.
The deepening evening sends
long shadows outward from the poolside furniture,
as if to fill the empty places left here,

and I suddenly think of my last night with you,
how we could change or stave off nothing,
and the way your hand traveled over my back.

Apocrypha

One argued that the manuscript
could not be authentic. It lacked spirit.

One stressed that the word they had translated
as *earth* should be, in fact, *clay*.

Another agreed that such attention
was important, but that at this time deviated
from the intent of their inquest.

Soon they forgot the fragmented Scripture
as each interrupted the other.

The one standing column, which stood
at the edge of what they believed
to be the edge of the city,
counted the hours.
                    Its shadow
lengthened and shortened and lengthened.

Midsummer Vestments

If a line of thought is followed
long enough, it leads to laughter.
There beside the garage, in the gray

thin shade of noon, is the argument
of greenness, the fern's uncurling,
a hesitant flowering.

The truth is that there comes a time
when day divides into unequal
portions—midsummer, for instance,

the sun over the overworked lawns,
the half-moon falling more quickly
than it rose, pulling down with it

the threadbare breeze.
In the short nights, constellations
wind through their rhetoric. By August,

what remains of the fern is brittle,
a cartilaginous filigree,
a yellow lacework of remains,

the ruined architecture of the thing,
an arched and worthless fragility.
Given two choices, one is lament.

News of the World

They told me the news
And I hung up the phone
And I knew
I would have to keep it simple
I went to my room
And counted my cash
I had four hundred dollars
Which I put in my pocket
I went to my closet
And changed my shoes
And put on a clean shirt
I stood at the mirror
And combed my hair
Then I put on my coat
And went downstairs
And got a cab
To the airport

Meeting

Color is not close to what they are saying.
The elevator goes over and through the doors,
palm trees shift their weight in glass.
Noise is shaped like paper clips falling
on white carpet.

Her eyes are so thick and shiny
she can't tell what he is about to say.
The up and down is reflected, his hand
stretches over her knee, and millions
of staring girls wander by.

It's because she's wearing
a black dress
and he's in jeans.

But that's not all.

He looks airborne, as if
some aberration hovered in his skull.

It is not clear what they are saying,
but the arrangement has its brilliance.

Middle Age

What I can't decide
is where I am.
All these white chairs
between round white tables
are like the dining room
of a transatlantic liner.
The silver's precisely placed.
Four drained glasses. Too many
clean plates. It's all right,
I've worn my pearls.
The man across from me
has white hair and a white shirt.
The pasta is pale, shiny,
arranged with shrimp and pink salmon;
there's a lettuce leaf,
a purple mussel shell.
The people next to us
are known strangers.
We order one dessert.
You eat the pastry, I
the strawberries. One dry rose,
a blot of blood between us,
a huge tree dropping its leaves.

Volume Five

It's the only thing she doesn't describe.
A bomb fractures the bank of the river,
floods the monotonous meadow.

It's wild, fearful, the mirror pulling
down orange clouds with green behind,
Henry James saying, "Watch whatever's happening
to you."

She thinks she's written the last perfect sentence.
Ghosts are calling from dark to dark,
bridges break upstream.

She puts down her stick
and walks into the river, her pockets
pulled down with rocks.

She's given up light to look
at black trees wicking water underground.

It's deeper, thicker,
it keeps getting longer ago.

Two Boats

In the dark the green canoe
moves toward a light on shore.
How do I know that this rowboat,
heavy with packs and dog,
uncertain oarlocks creaking,
will reach land when
the paddler finishes his journey?

Blistered hands struggle
to light the water, the dog barks,
blue trees sprout from the packs.
I see a door cut in a cliff.
There's no shore.
No land. No docking place.
No green canoe.

Going to David's Party

David is stuffing blue flower petals
into a clear glass tube.
They cry out like butterfly wings.
He has come to invite them to a party.
It is over a hill and down a valley
full of quick rivers. They want to go,
but the door is open only a crack
and there is a long string holding them
to the top of the stairs. What
is on the end of the string?
It is a painting of what life
is supposed to be like. They fly
above it, green-leaved birds
turning blue from the sky.
A yellow lark rises from a fence post,
the river runs flamingo. There they are,
happy at the other door, ready to go in,
and there is David, holding a vase of larkspur.

Appeal

I will not go down,
but let me rot up here;

let my face slide off
slowly to the dramas

of the streeted world.
God, damn yourself

or let me off the hook,
for I have chomped hard

on leathery bread
and gulped bloody tears.

Take it from me,
you self-made bastard,

this penny-carnival
you set me down in

is a place unclean.
I am not your excrement.

I am not a lamb
patient for your sodomy.

I love my life.
Goddamnit, God bless it.

Haruspex

Fresh intestines drape
Traffic signals and flagpoles,
Clog sewers and mess up

Satellite transmissions—
They are everywhere.
Nothing has gone wrong.

The less we say the better.
John John scooped up ten
Pounds with a bucket.

It was all carefully planned.
No one had to go to war.
My wife returned home

With five full grocery bags.
I didn't ask questions.
Most birds stopped flying.

My colleagues understood.
My head ached eleven days
So I got out of my Toyota

And refused to get a girl.
The crowd went wild.
I got scared and looked up.

There was someone tall
In a brand-new bathing suit,
A tag dangling from his teeth.

I took a drag and spit spit.
Then the ground dropped away.
Hallelujah. I said hallelujah.

Waiting Room

Rick, my upstairs neighbor, hacked open his
     living-room floor
with his girlfriend Sandy, and threw her through
     the hole,
yelling, "Where did you hide my riboflavin,
     goddamnit? All
I ask for in life are the full recommended daily
     allowances."

Sandy hit my floor, looked up, and answered his
     question.
"Rick, did you check next to your thiamin? I'm
     almost positive
I put your riboflavin next to your thiamin." It was
     my turn
to say something, so I said to her, "Do you know
     that it costs
less than twenty-five cents to produce a 75-watt
     light bulb,
and yet we are forced to cough up two dollars for
     each one?"

Outside, a wind began to blow furiously and detach
     many leaves
from the available branches. I was summarily
     unimpressed
and continued to speak. "Also, too many people
     think it unsafe
to eat fruit from dented cans, when the fact of the
     matter is clear:

fruit from dented cans poses no threat whatsoever
  to the consumer.
But the widespread, irrational fear of all foods from
  dented cans
forces the unfortunate store owners to set up
  special discount bins
which allow the intelligent consumers to save on
  their grocery bills."

Rick called down to Sandy, "I found the bottle,
  Sandy! I'm sorry
I overreacted!" Sandy answered: "That's okay,
  honey, I shouldn't tidy up!
And will you please throw down a rope, this man is
  out of his mind."

Ars Poetica

Let us beat up people
wearing glasses,
pluck out their lenses
and arrange them
in a paper-towel tube
so that we can observe
high heaven in the way
of the first astronomers.

Let us farm the dead
and gobble maggots
blindfolded, with our hands
tied behind our backs,
and position our assholes
on the points of steeples
and spin around like toys.

Let us forget to wipe
the smirks from our faces.

Notes to Daedalus

1. They talk of knowledge
but the sun
is just an orb.

2. I would go if I could.

3. Sometimes we fall.

The Kiss

Our mouths fit
perfectly sealed
like an airlock.
The only thing
protecting us
from the chill
vacuum outside
is our own breath.

Romantic Love, 1987

It's best this way: you, a winding staircase
in a nineteenth-century monastery;
me, a pack of Lucky Strikes
wadded up, empty, purely decorative now.

But, hey—

A. P. CRUMLISH

Fire

The fire was started by a spark
igniting coconut husk
fiber in a cushion maker's house.

Several people die each year on country roads.
Returning inebriated from taverns,
body heat depleted by alcohol,
they are drawn to warm macadam.
They lie down.
Four out of five drivers stop.
Some are run over more than once.

The fire was started by a spark
igniting coconut husk
fiber in a cushion maker's house.

They applaud as the hearse drives by.
Victim's father witnesses the execution,
fulfilling the promise of the day
his son was buried.

The fire was started by a spark
igniting coconut husk
fiber in a cushion maker's house.

Archbishop orders fifty-four Templars
burned at the stake
for retracting confessions.
Bearded man stops at the center of the bridge.
He is assigned to the work crews.
He watches two infants and a woman

placed on a grill
over a fiery pit.

The fire was started by a spark
igniting coconut husk
fiber in a cushion maker's house.

Ellis Island

Never had spaghetti before coming to America.
It took twelve days.
Botany Hill. Mr. Lang.
Always very nice to me, that Mr. Lang.
Coming to America.
Didn't see the statue.
Never had spaghetti before coming to America.
It took twelve days.
Doesn't choke, it fattens you.
Two plus two.
I could do long division by decimals.
Night school. Mr. Lang.
Always very nice to me, that Mr. Lang.
Coming to America.
It took twelve days.
Must have been a lot of chickens in America,
I thought,
passing shacks and shacks crossing New Jersey.
Didn't see the statue.
Can't talk but can explain what it means.
It took twelve days,
coming to America.
I never had spaghetti before coming to America.

Laundry

Sunday night she bends over the bed
and folds the flat ghosts of her children.
Shoulders doubled back to their waists,
arms bent over chests; bottoms halved,
crotches tucked to the center. She stacks
them in neat piles in drawers and recalls
her mother folding up her life, hands on her lap
waiting for the hinged top of the coffin to close.
Tonight her mind is like the crust of the earth,
creased and furrowed, or a wave tucking
into itself before land. Whenever
space bends, great distances are lost.
She looks at her hands and sees time
falling between the folds of her skin.

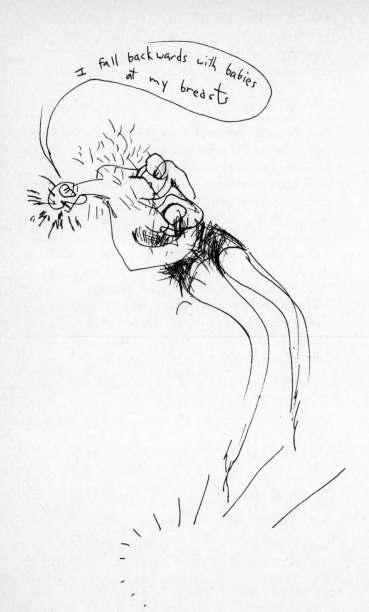

International House of Hunan Pancake (Breakfast deliver all day)

SOUP

Runny Egg on Plate That Look Like Soup 1.05
Hot and Sour Soup. 1.00
Hot and Nice Soup. 1.00
Not Hot Soup 1.00
Soup with Mood and Temp of Choice. 2.00

APPETIZER

Chicken Wing 4.75
Fried Chicken Thing. 2.00
Crispy "Happy-Face" Pancake with Egg, Rib, and Pineapple
   Chunk (with Tea or Syrup). 4.50
Rib. 4.75
Feet (price according to size) . . . .
Aromatic Spare Feet. 4.75
Two-Delicacy Cold Cut 5.00

SWEET AND SOUR

Sweet and Sour. 6.50
Sweet and Sour Cream. 5.50
Sweet and Sour Grape 5.75
Sweet and Sour Fork 6.50
Sweet and Sour Junket. 7.50

EGG FOO
(served with 3 Pancake or Noodle Hunan Style)

Egg Foo 4.50

NOODLE, RICE

Cold Noodle. 3.00
Old Noodle with Warm Hot Sauce. 3.50

Fried "Weiss" Rice (with Nova Scotia Salmon Shreds and
    Cream Cheese) 7.00

CHICKEN

Snow-Shoe Chicken 6.50
Hack Chicken in Assorted Syrup.................... 4.50
Stab Chicken 4.50
Killed Chicken in Open-Casket-Basket
    for All World to See 5.00

DUCK

Hiding Duck...................................... 7.50
Crispy Syrupy Duck............................... 8.00

DESSERT

Chunk (one)...................................... 1.00
Fortunate Cookie................................. 1.00
Unfortunate Cookie .... .95
Whole Sauteed Spice 2.00
Ice Creamy Bean Curd with Dark Brown .... .95
Kumquat (stuffed) 1.75
Blintz (with Snow Pea)............................ 2.25
Cake Betty (Pie with Choice of Rib,
    Wing, or Sugar, Baked Brown) 2.75

Detti Detti, is it really you on this moldy postcard (advertising *Imren Cikolatasi*) that I dug out of a dusty shoebox from a hole-in-a-wall notions shop in Izmir, Turkey? Yes, yes, who can doubt that lustrous hair in a half-upsweep so reminiscent of those hard peroxides of forties stardom, but softened on you, Detti Casoli, famous *Italyan Artisti,* by your angelic Grable–De Havilland face that could pout like Shirley Temple's and "express the emotional range of Lassie"—that last remark so cruel, so untrue, and the critic happily long dead and forgotten, unlike you, Detti Casoli, in that notorious black silk swimsuit loosely corseted from breast to belly with thin strings of Mama Casoli's homemade linguini. "Do you have an appetite, boys?" And that swimsuit specially designed for you by Giovanni Gritti for that sensational bulb-popping stroll across the Ponte Vecchio as Dante's new Beatrice . . . And that fabulous Casoli smile like a slice of sweet *meloni* floating above the steep and creamy-white twin peaks of Monte Detti (where it was said to be so high, the air had no air to breathe, and died). Of course, you are pushing forty in this faded *fotografia,* and perhaps a bit porky, but never you mind, my lovely Detti, your Pepsodenti teeth are as pearly as ever, set in the luscious blood-oval of your lips (painted always to fire-engine perfection). "Without my lipstick I am naked," you once confessed, and just to imagine this sets off sirens in my head: *Detti burns down Roma by merely smiling!* Ah, how you captured the swifts of imagination and hawks of desire! Look at that irresistible foto drop you carried everywhere—how the boards simulate a gate about to swing out on a billowy sea, inviting us to dive in with you, Detti, for sunny frolicking, and the hordes of young men who drowned to be seaworthy with you on the long swim to your villa on the Isle of Capri (where it was rumored that hairy

İTALYAN DETTİ ARTİSTİ CASOLI

İMREN Çikolatası

bruto hubby of yours did not fulfill your needs and regularly beat you). And that inimitable Detti trademark, there it is, the Chinese coolie hat with its wide round brim uplifted, encircling your head like a halo of pizza or a planetary system. How perfect, how *simpatico* for space-age generations to come and the opening of Western relations with China! You were ahead of your time, Detti, my Mona Lisa of bathing-beauty queens and Prophetissa of the Future. From spiked heels to golden upsweep, your body stands as a question mark and answer: *Beauty,* which is Truth, according to Keats, *wedded to political conviction.* And here you are again, my lovely Detti, hands behind your back, holding the secret gift for those who dare to come swim with you. I dared, Detti, and as one of the drowned in your faded and sun-drenched past, I send up this last bubble of memory to you, *Detti Detti*! **Q**

Today is my anniversary. Would have been twenty-nine years. So deep down all week. Death is no event, it is just ever after. It is finding his shoes in the closet. It is knowing that no one will ever be him. Today is gray and snowing light. There is a wind from off the lake, so snowflakes look like floating up. This has been the most godawful week. Friday, good old friend, drinking buddy, comes over at four-thirty in morning, suitcase packed, wanting booze. I give her tea. Go out Saturday night to cowboy bar owned by my girl friend Vivian, who reads cards. We meet millionaire, seventeen times he tells me. I tell him I pack blower motors for a living. David and I come down to office six-thirty each morning. We are in serious trouble. Will know by next month if we can continue. We are not the smart my husband was. Last week sold one thousand battery chargers. Sharon Olds! God, she is wonderful; can write about anything, making love while bleeding. Note how I get back to sex. Friend sends me book with odd devices, rubber things, some with chipmunks on. Catalogue makes me cry. Read it, anyway. Purse-size devices you can carry along. We have sixteen people on the payroll and need all because of assembly. Oh, liked last issue, story about toilet paper and R. Bass's last. Only person asks me for a real date is the bell captain at favorite hotel. A sixty-year-old bellboy. I almost said yes. Do you think I'm going crazy? Please don't feel sorry for me. As you can see, I have a million men. They're just not men. Want to see what's in my purse? The stems of the tulips are reaching up. Flowers return, unlike people, and make me cry. Everything seems to make me cry. Raven calls me other day, had a bout with rheumatic fever over Christmas, hair fell out, now all back more black, more thick than ever. He says, "What will I do now if I live?" The drama of his AIDS has been his life for years. I laugh, but it is just the question I ask myself each day. Monday used to be my favorite day of the week. Monday is so very hard now. After playing cards all weekend with his seventy-year-old friends, who complained of headaches and no more sex, Harold wanted to prove to me he was not like them. Or prove to himself. So on Monday he went all-out. I meanwhile now am out stumbling somewhere around town the other night; had too much champagne at party in my old building. Going home, I climb fence to cut across parking lot; climbing second fence I fall, luckily by the Rehab Center. Man in wheelchair comes over, pulls me up with long, strong arms. Wheels home with me. Keeps asking, "Are you all right?" I'm okay, but him, him? Ellie's house is all white and mirrors. She washes walls already clean. My son David and I work all Easter weekend, stay overnight at plant, have big order to go out Monday. Maybe we can make it; still don't know. Slept on floor where rats run around. Packed four thousand blower motors almost alone. I don't want to remarry. I have nothing to give to anybody. Cannot even give myself. Just had call from our landlord. Hear my sons try to lie. Tell him I can't pay him, am trying to save ourselves here. Feel like offstage mother screaming, "The landlord is coming!" It's sex I want, but miss more the constant constant constant touch of safe skin of him. Morning is the worst. Wake up so damn alone. If it weren't for the kids needing me, would move to Europe. Easier being alone there. Live in one mean room and on the street. These friends of mine, they neither read nor write. Where do they put things? I have taken a vow of chastity, so, of course, I fell in love ten times this week. Went to early dinner with old friends of Harold and mine—Cookie and Earl and Harold went to high school together. This is the first time I have seen any of the people we knew as couples; they call me, but I have not been able to see them. Seeing them together drove me straight into the bed of a stranger, where I spent the night making a sort of half-love. At dinner, I was bright and wonderful with my friends. Talked about old times. Told them my plans. They probably think, Oh, Sharon, she is doing so well. They want me to come to their place in the suburbs and look at old pictures—Harold and me and the kids at the zoo, at Disneyland, at weddings. Tell them I will. Know I won't. Made teenage love all night long. Made me come with his fingers and his tongue. Fingers covered with blood. Bed is covered with blood. Go into the bathroom to clean myself. In the mirror I see woman, old and crying, blood dripping down legs, smear on my cheek. He comes in and stands behind me, lifts my breasts. "Can you come again?" Gets washcloth and washes more of it off my legs. I want to go home. I want to get home before David wakes up. I am taking pills to sleep. Cried when I came. Two months ago, Shelby had a mastectomy; reconstruction at the same time. Shelby says two nights ago Spiro kissed her scars, told Shelby he didn't mind the missing nipple, that she was beautiful. Shelby pulls her blouse up and shows us the scars. We move the candle on the restaurant table closer; the scars are under and above a deep angry purple. She says they're going to make a nipple from her cunt. "That's not bad," I say. "Look at mine." I pull my blouse up. I hate my stretch marks, like varicose veins. Georgie shows us her breasts, which are beautiful (she has implants). Ellie's breasts are so big she has to wear matron bras or her jugs hang to her waist. Judy comes over and screams, "What are you dumb old broads doing! Are you nuts! Jesus Christ!" We forgot. Later our sons come and take us crying, crying home. **Q**

Lish asked me to write a page about myself. I'm from New Mexico, the dryest part. Everyone seems interested when I tell them where I was born its my most unique quality. I've always felt that some revelation should have been given to me coming from such a place where no one in their right mind would live. We moved alot. My mom still does. My dad built a house and planted two trees when I was born then abandoned it because he couldn't grow a soda lawn. ~~they~~ ~~I loved riding~~ all day in a car. my teeth resting on the metal window frame so the vibration of the car would rattle my entire head. Something kept us in the west. I grew up surrounded by cowboys and Indians in northern nebraska. We rarely saw them. I put on my letter jacket and felt I like another american. I never lettered in anything.

"I'll never make it" my most common thought. it controlls everything I do,

I Loved ranching. I broke my tailbone rounding up cows. I yi yippee I yow

I took art in college. I worked in factories

I did substitute teaching in chikago. It was so tense that I nearly threw up every day when the final bell rang and I could relax.

I went back to new mexico and ~~changed tires~~ changed tires for a minimum wage. After wounded knee I made Indian jewelry.

I came to N.Y.C. everything ~~got better~~ got better I think

Don Nace